TRAGEDY AND TRIUMPH

The Tragic Yet Triumphant Autobiography and Memoirs of One Man's Immigration Journey to America

Dominic Merola

Table of Contents

Preface

What you are about to read is a true story. I have been carrying it in my head for decades. Every time I felt like putting it on paper, I would somehow change my mind. Now, the time has come to put it on paper. Maybe it is because of my age, or maybe it is because many people have urged me to do so. This story involves my early life. It was eventful, to say the least.

As a young man I suddenly found myself on the way to America just before my sixteenth birthday -- all to fulfill my family's dream. Everything seemed to run as planned at the beginning. Even though I had recently lost a dear member of my family and the pain was still fresh in my memory, life had to go on.

It began on October 1, 1952. It was only a few days before my 16th birthday. I was informed that I had to make it to America before my birthday had passed in order to become a citizen there. It was not easy to do but my family scrounged up the money and paid for me to fly to the USA. Alone, I hoped that although there were many obstacles in my way and some unexpected events as well, I concentrated on another family member who planned to follow me to America. I was elated that my brother Alfonso might soon follow and join me.

Yet, not long after arriving in America, I contracted an unexpected and serious viral infection that nearly took my life. I held on through the illness, knowing that I would no longer be alone after I recovered.

The illness set me back. I started high school about two months late due to my illness. I struggled to catch up to the other students in my freshman year. By late March of 1954 I got some somber news from home. My brother Alfonso had been in an accident while digging for sand alone one fateful day. The side of the pit gave way and he was trapped. Help came too late to revive him and he died. At this point, my family abandoned hope of coming to America.

What was I now to do? I had to ask myself if I was tough enough to stay alone in America. I also felt a sense of responsibility to return to Italy and help my shattered family. After all the sacrifices that were made on my behalf, what was I to do with my own situation?

I started school late back home in Italy because the war had thrown everything into chaos. I worked diligently and carried a heavy curriculum to bring me up to par with the other teenagers that were starting about two to three grades ahead of me. Then suddenly I was uprooted to come to America to keep my family's dream alive. That's when tragedy struck. I had to make a difficult decision. Should I leave high school in America and return home to an unknown future, or should I tough it out alone in America?

I will aim to explain all these situations and reveal how it all turned out -- and how so many things worked in mysterious ways to arrive to the outcome described in later chapters. I hope not to give the impression that all I am doing is feeling sorry for myself. There are others who have had to endure more serious situations than me. Everyone sees their own trials and errors. How do you even begin to compare them to the lives of others?

Each person has his or her story. Some choose to be silent about it. For some, talking about it is part of a healing process. Others feel a compelling desire to write it down. For others, it's a desire to simply share their experience with the readers. For me it's various reasons that I keep to myself. Let's just say that I think it is good to put these life experiences on paper.

Since childhood I have done things that the average person will never experience in their lifetime. Not because I am smarter or possess special talents or skills. It's a matter of circumstances. I hope to tell my story because I have had this compelling desire to do it. Individuals have urged me many times to write about my experiences in life. These experiences may not be the most monumental or of great consequence to some, yet I think that they are unique in many respects. Maybe I can show someone a different spin on how life can be in another country or continent. Maybe I can remind a young person that life did exist before such things as satellite television, iPhones, and the Internet.

I know what it's like to endure a major war, family tragedies, and at the same time fight the demons that I had to fight to go on with life. While I never claimed to have talents beyond my normal abilities, I did just want to say how things were and still are today in some measure.

Life, I learned a long time ago, is a struggle with valleys and peaks. The way we react to it is the big difference. At times I have fought the good fight. Other times I had to have the patience of Job. I can say with certainty that I have tried to do good. I have received some good in return. Many times I was not so lucky. That's just the way it goes.

These are a few important things that I am trying to portray or pass on to the readers, if possible. In the following chapters I will attempt to bring you to the memories that have formed in my mind and try to present them the best way I know. After all, I am but an ordinary person with an unusual set of circumstances.

It's a shame that both my parents, although American-born, had to live without their dream of coming back to America. My father visited me for about six months in the mid-1970's. My mother never saw her birthplace again.

I dedicate this book to my family. First, to my brother Elio. He was by far the closest to me -- my mentor, my friend, and my hero. He was instrumental in my continued education. I was the first to achieve that goal. Back then, before WWII, living in the rural areas, not very many farmers attended high school. Many had to make due with night school if they were lucky.

I also dedicate this book to my brother Alfonso. He was the "English Lord," or so my father used to call him. After I came to America, he was to follow me. Due to the untimely death of Leo, Al was next in line to communicate with me. Before we could become close like Leo and me, I lost him to an untimely death.

My brother Joseph was more of the easygoing type. He was involved in commerce. In our community, you could ask for "Peppe" (Giuseppe) for whatever you needed to sell or buy. Sometimes he would take me with him. He would pretend to make me figure the costs, sale prices, and so on, just to amuse me. He would even allow me to earn some spending money. He was the oldest and more like a father figure. He also survived a prison camp in Germany. He had served in the Italian Army and was captured by the Germans. He became a prisoner of war and spent the last few years of the war in that camp. Every time I watch the television show, *Hogan's Heroes,* it makes me think of him.

My sister Mena (Philomena) was three years older than myself. We fought like cats and dogs. Still, we were "brother and sister" and remained close. I have to credit my parents, from whom this entire story originates -- without them there would be no story. They were American by birth, both of them, with a wish to live once again in America. They never realized that dream.

First of all I must thank my daughter-in-law, Tressa, for taking on the task of transcribing this entire story from a manuscript to print, along with her husband, my son, Chris, for helping to make some final edits, enhancements, and the necessary refining touches to it.

I also want to thank my oldest son, John, for helping to get this story published. Finally, I want to express my gratitude to the Struthers School Board for keeping the international radio program airing on WKTL. Listening to the Italian hour hosted by Joe Mazzocca and his son brought back many memories and provided me with inspiration to pen my story. This is my story.

Chapter 1: The Early Years

Sometimes in life, a life-threatening event happens and we have a moment of instant replay. It is then that our life flashes in front of our eyes. I think most of us have experienced such moments -- when we have a car accident, a fall or other sudden scary event. As we enter the autumn of our life, we drift into a mode of review, of how we have lived. How did we get here from childhood? Sometimes music awakens the memories of when we first heard that piece -- and even what we were doing and our surroundings. It is just such a thing that brings me back to where I grew up.

My story begins during a period that overlaps from the pre-World War II and post-World War II era. It seems like just yesterday, but when I stop to think about it, it is more decades that have passed than I want to admit. My place of birth is an area that most resembles a large rectangle. It runs length-wise north and south and the width runs from east and west. At a glance, you could even think that it is closed on the four corners, as a closed-in valley. However, if you look closely or drive to the four corners you find ample space on all four sides.

On the northwest corner, a mountain jots

southeast into that corner as a short tangent. As it slopes down, it becomes finely flat into the village center. The old part of town was founded on both sides of the slope. The center of the village is on level ground. The valley's length is about ten to fifteen miles long, while the width is six to eight miles wide, both east and west. The river Volturno runs south, about half way between the two long sides of the valley. Along the east and the west sides of the valley's foothills, small towns and villages cling to the base of these mountains, mostly close to the main roads. My town is located on the northwest corner, as I mentioned above. It is called Baia. The twin town Latina is about two miles south, along the Provincial Road. From my birth to the day I left it, this is what I knew.

Why were these small towns built on the mountain sides? It was primarily for self-defense. There could be several other reasons. First, when a baron or other person of influence was given a large tract of land, they wanted to protect it from numerous rogue armies or other rivals. Before there were stable, established nations, this was a prevalent practice all over Europe. Different tribes and marauding armies would swoop in from nowhere and attack and plunder such villages. This is why every village had a tall tower over the highest point of that village. This was to help identify an enemy before they came too close to their town.

Our town, Baia, has such a tower. It still stands, although it is in poor shape these days. Many times I took refuge in it when I was watching sheep and it was very windy.

According to a local booklet printed by the municipal building records, it was built by the Longobards, a Germanic tribe that invaded the area between the sixth and eighth centuries. When I was there last time, in September 2012, it was in restoration mode. Our sister city, Latina, also has a tower. It is in better condition than ours. According to the same source, it was built by the Latins or Romans probably earlier yet.

I have my own theory about it. It may have been that the lords owned the land. The peasants that they hired to work the land had to build on the mountain slopes. The plots were free of charge and the building materials were there and ready to be used. It just may be that was the case. Some even theorize that in those days people valued fresh air and up high there was more of it. Ultimately, no one today really knows for sure what happened. It is just amazing that those buildings have withstood the test of time for centuries.

The streets built with cobblestones are still in good shape today. There are some buildings that are being remodeled and modernized for those people who appreciate that type of antiquity. Another benefit from that type of village is that when it rains, the whole community looks bleached from the water that runs down on each terraced street. You might even say that they had a self-cleaning city -- and there was no waste of energy by the people.

Nowadays, people have built beautiful houses there down on the level ground. Along new streets and roads, there are still some people that live up on the high slopes of the mountains. Some of those roads have now been blacktopped to enable cars to go where cobblestone and terraced streets were. It's nice that cars can travel way to the top of these villages, but the charm of antique cobblestone with small terraced steps every so often is gone.

From what I was able to observe as of two years ago, only the very highest parts were abandoned. You would have to see for yourself how quaint some of these homes and apartments have been made. Sometimes you see the old and new merge in such a way that makes one marvel at the ingenuity with which they are fashioned. I have been in some of these and they are quite comfortable. The way they were made originally, walled in as condos, they can be cool through the summer and warm in the winter. Every small group of homes and apartments has their own bottegas and tiny shops.

While there in Italy in 2012, I noticed that every Friday, part of the village's streets becomes a mercato (market). You can buy everything under the sun there, from produce to fruit to jewelry. I almost felt like I could love living there once again.

Rarely as a child did I go to other cities, except Latina, which I visited mostly in the summers when they had festivals. On a clear day you could see the whole valley. It was peaceful and steady. The sky was usually blue. I was too young then to have any worries. This was my peaceful valley. It was happy and serene. I could look around at that panorama and inhale it. I felt that what I could see was mine to enjoy. It was part of me. I could own it anytime I looked up. This and much more comes to me when I hear songs of that era. I can be there mentally. I can envision it and feel the bliss of that innocent time. I can hear my brothers sing, especially Alfonso. He was good at it. He had a fantastic voice.

There were also hardships in these small towns, as there are in every country, much like the ones that we have in America. In my experience, some of the people who have the least are the happiest, like those who live in the Appalachian region, where conditions sometimes are not as good as the rest of the country. Based on my observation, some of the people who live there seem to be more joyous even though they live with much less materially. Music is a big part of their life and probably a way to forget their struggles. Their styles of music might even be somewhat different from the rest of nation, but they miss it even when they move on to a new life in the more industrialized centers. It makes me think of artists such as John Denver, with his song, "Country Road Take Me Home."

Am I saying that I was better off there in that small village? Do I have regrets of coming to America? No, not at all. We are the envy of the world here in America. Just as an adopted child cannot forget about his or her birth mother and will always seek to see her at least sometime during life, I am drawn to my birth place again.

It grieves me to think of the hardships that some villagers endured just to survive. They worked so hard to eke out a living from the fields they tilled, mostly with older instruments and bare hands. Tractors and other machinery were owned by landlords and the rich farmers during the reign of Mussolini's fascism. It was only after the war ended and Mussolini was removed that their plight began to improve, as evidenced by the fact that Italy is a member of the G-8 trade partnership today.

Still, there was a lot of singing, joking, and laughter during those hard times. It seemed that everyone sang or whistled. Music and song was ever present. This brings to mind a tale that I heard. There once was a couple that was rich and lived near a shoemaker. The rich couple was more or less lonely. The shoemaker sang all day long, often annoying the rich couple. One day, the rich couple decided to drop a large bag of money down to the shoemaker through a doorway. They observed the shoemaker soon stopped singing. Funny, how money changes your perspective on life.

During the summer months in my hometown, there were feasts almost every month to celebrate. In addition to these festivities, the neighboring villages and towns had their own feasts and celebrations. In my family, my brothers had a record player for a time. Being the youngest of five I absorbed all my knowledge of music from my siblings. By far my brother Alfonso was most up on all the new songs. He had a great voice. He was the second eldest and very much a ladies' man. Some girls used to ask me about him constantly. "Where is he?" they would ask. They would inquire, "Where is he working today and who is he dating now?" It always made me feel so good to know that my brother was so popular. I was very proud of him and the others as well. Each of them had their own special gifts and talents that I appreciated.

Some of the best times that I recollect were when we exchanged days of work with other families and friends. This was always done throughout the year. By far, it was most used during harvest. In early summer there were fields of golden wheat. How beautiful to see golden wheat fields waving in gentle breezes. It was almost a shame to harvest that beauty, moving in the wind like rhythms and waves. Larger farms had combines for harvesting wheat. The smaller and more numerous farms were the private family farms. They employed workers who wielded sickles. Usually, there were large groups wearing mostly straw hats which were lightweight, promoted ventilation, and provided shade to the head and shoulders. Even while they performed hard labor, they usually sang, joked, and shared in the laughter.

Once the wheat was cut and laid down in large separate bunches, then came the tying of the wheat in sheaves. Often, the workers would play "Morra" and the loser would tie the winner's sheaf. Morra is played by one player throwing out a number of fingers while saying the total of his, plus what he or she anticipates the other will throw. Whoever comes out with the right total wins. The loser would have to tie the sheaves of the winner, plus his own.

After the workers used the thrashing machines where the wheat is separated from the husk and the straw, they would again work together as a group. Just as before, laughter and joking continued as they worked. I liked to watch the machines, especially the steam engine that powered the thrashing machines.

Our Volturno River was another asset to the community. It ran southward almost half way between the east and west sides of the valley. It ran clear like a crystal. There were many types of fish and eels in the river, including clams. We often went swimming in it, especially after working in the fields. We did not drink from it though; after all, animals would drink its water and often could also relieve themselves into it.

Coming upon the river was always exciting. I always got butterflies in my stomach as I neared its banks. Rushing currents were fun to watch. There were deep whirlpools that I feared too. The constant sounds of water movements were in harmony with frogs and birds chirping and nesting. Song birds were my favorites, especially the "Merla," with its bright yellow bills and distinctive harmonious songs. So beautiful are their songs that the radio stations often use these as chimes, just before a broadcast or news. It is considered a European Robin, except that its color is fully black with a yellow bill. You could also call it Merlo for male and Merla for female, or Merli, the plural of both. Interestingly, this Merla bird appears to be where my family derived its last name, Merola. It was taken from the formal Italian language.

Now living in Western Pennsylvania, I am privileged to hear some of the songs I heard growing up come to me from across the border in Ohio, over WKTL through the Italian program. When I hear the beautiful and poetic songs of Carlo Buti, Luciano Vergilio, Claudio Villa, Caruso, and other artists of that era, I am brought back to that time of innocence when I was young. I think mostly about Carlo Buti of Florence, known as the "Golden Voice of Italy" with his popular folk-style songs of the day and his melodic tenor style. It's as if I can breathe the air and see the blue skies. I can imagine it and inhale the surroundings. There I feel at peace; if just for a moment.

I was born in 1936, on October fourth. I learned that it was a cool and misty morning in Baia, about forty-five to fifty miles northeast of Naples and about thirty-five miles from Caserta, the province and capital. My father's Zia (Aunt) Concetta had been at my parents' farm, assisting the midwife. As my mother was giving birth to me, the fifth and last in my family, Zia Concetta was making her way to her small apartment when she confided with her neighbor, Rachele Conte, about my birth. She told her that her niece had given birth to a boy and spoke of "what a large head he has." The strange coincidence is that twenty-two years later, three thousand miles and one continent away, I will be reunited with Rachele's family in a way that changed my life. Even stranger, we would later become family, as you will see later on.

Our farm was located less than two miles from our sister village of Latina. The two villages share a municipality, as well as a cemetery. The main road is the Provincial Road, running north and south along the foothills of the west side of the valley. It links other villages at the foothills north and south of Baia. It is here, on that same road, about a quarter mile from the village, that Sal and Maria, my parents, with their five children, made their home on a small family farm. I was the youngest. Then came my sister Mena; she was three years older. Before Mena was born, my parents had Elio, who was about 10 years older than me. Alfonso was 13 years my senior and Joe was the eldest, 15 years older than me.

It must have been around 1940, when I was about four years old, that I began to have my most lasting memories. At that time, Mussolini was involved with Germany and entered WW II in June of 1940. I remember riding on the oxen driven cart. We had fodder for our animals, as we neared our farm. There were church bells ringing in town and a lot of commotion. My mother began to cry. Joseph, my brother, had been drafted by the Italian army. She knew he would face danger. This was as controversial to the Italian majority as the Vietnam War was to the American people during the late 1960's. My mother's fears were realized. It wasn't too much longer when Joe was eventually sent to fight in Greece. It was a scary time for my family.

I will never forget these events of my childhood. They are so vivid even now. They remain clear as a bell in my mind. Social scientists call times like this "impact events." They make such an impact that you will never forget them. These are the memories that have lasted a lifetime.

My next memory is my being in the kitchen one morning. We all slept in bedrooms upstairs. The kitchen area, on the first floor, was the central gathering place, usually by the fireplace. I being the youngest was often left alone with my mother as she finished the breakfast dishes. On this particular morning I was alone. Outside I heard something so powerfully beautiful. I still cannot describe how delightfully pleasing to my young ears it was. I was smitten with its sound. It was a piano forte (organ grinder). What was more mysterious was the parrot that was with him. It was asked to pick out my brother Elio's fortune from a ream of charts. I thought for sure that what the parrot picked out was my brother's specific chart. And how did he know which one to pick? I was mesmerized by it all. In retrospect, this reminds me of the children in the story of the "Pied Piper."

Across the river and east of our farm, a chain of mountains stood a few miles high. The peaks would be snowcapped until late June and early July. It is called Monte Matese. I recall the sun emerging from behind the peaks of Monte Matese, directly east of our farm's facade. It would warm the chill in the morning air. Usually Zio Luigi (Uncle Lou) would take his morning strolls. He came from the village with his cane. He was a tall, slender gentleman, always upbeat. He often would bring us the latest bit of news or gossip from the village. A retired masonry worker with a slightly high pitched voice and small mustache, he often would walk my sister to school. After the fire at the fireplace went out by late morning, I would venture out and bask in the sun for warmth.

Not long after these events, I began to see military vehicles pass by. We were no more than thirty feet or so from the Provincial Road. As such, I was tuned in to all the activities. People going and coming from a good portion of the countryside would pass by our farm.

Running right across our farm was a central country road that led to most of the fields east and south of the village. In addition, the farmers of that same area came via that country road, which led to the Provincial Road. It led them to the villages or towns, both north and south. I had no idea that a war was beginning, let alone where and with whom. Only the adults knew. I only knew that Joe, my brother, was a soldier. It was only later, while listening to the adults talking about the war, that I began to make some sense of things.

Once in a while, my mother would take me to the village to kindergarten class. I used to hate it with a passion. Call it separation anxiety or whatever it was, but I had almost no contact with the other children of my age except Josephine -- daughter to our neighbors just a quarter mile east. She would walk me to kindergarten classes sometimes. I remember carrying a wicker lunch box. Once, I had an apple in it. I think it was a Macintosh. I learned to hate its smell. Even now, those apples remind me of that school that I hated so much.

Josephine was just about two or three years older than me. Another young girl about my age was Marietta, a niece to the neighbors across the road. Other than these, I don't remember any other playmates. This may have had something to do with my feeling uncomfortable in class. Besides, they were city slickers as far as I was concerned. I was from the farm. It never occurred to me that these other students were also children of farmers like me in most instances.

As time passed and I was a bit older, my brother Elio began to bring me along with him while he was pasturing our sheep. Elio was always my closest mentor in the family. Going out with him was so exciting. I would see new places on the mountains and in the countryside. He was about ten years older than me. I felt so lucky and important to have him to myself for days at a time. We grew closer during that period of time. Unbeknownst to me, that was really a training period for me. Those times were meant to familiarize me with sheep tending.

As the war came closer and intensified, my brother Al would also be drafted into the military service. Elio had to move up and take Al's place, taking on greater responsibilities. He now would be responsible for our cattle and actually plowing and farming with my father. Later, he was called upon to fill the vacuum that Joe and Al had left behind. I was gradually left alone more often with the sheep.

At first I hated going it alone. Even though I cared for the sheep by myself, Elio was either around with the cattle, among the other teenagers, or their animals. I liked being with the teenagers. They were fun to be around. There were times when they would get in trouble too. It was usually nothing terrible, just silly mischief. Sometimes they would go and raid someone's cherry tree, or play cards for money. On such an occasion, two Carabinieri (police) came upon them and caught them in the act of their mischief. They took them toward their station to book them. I began crying for Elio and his friends. I was really afraid of what would happen to them. Within half an hour they all came back. The police had let them go. They just wanted to strike some fear into their hearts. For a little boy like me it was terrifying.

When I became old enough, probably about six years of age, I would take the sheep out to pasture and head out on the west side of the town. I would go near the slope that jots on the northwest side of the rectangle that finishes in town. For a time my sister, who was about nine years old, would come to check on me after school. The area where I roamed was safe then. Everyone knew each other. As time went on, I started to feel confident on my own, except for those times when suddenly my sheep would disappear. At times they used to go after acorns on other people's property. Once I got my ears literally pulled back by the land owner for their transgression. He enjoyed it. He was really mean! I was afraid to tell my family. They would not have liked hearing that sometimes I dozed off while on the job. I didn't want them to scold me after all.

Then there was Giovanni, a man somewhat mentally challenged. He would stand in the middle of the road that led to my way home. He would threaten us as kids. He would stop us from passing. He was scary but not dangerous. I hated passing there. Even though he didn't harm anyone, he was a large man. To a six-year-old, he seemed like a giant. We saw it as a challenge to run away from the giant man and find our way home. He would utter, "You want to bet that I won't let you pass?"

As I approached the later part of my sixth year of life, the war was getting closer to my town. Rumors were spreading about the violence and casualties. I knew if the war came to my town that things would never be the same again for us. All I could do was hope that we were safe from it all.

The war did come finally to our town.

Chapter 2: The Summer of 1943

1943 was a busy year for me. There was a lot of crazy activity that year, beginning with the crash of an American bomber plane. I think it was a B-24 or something in that series. It happened during the late part of the night, almost before dawn. There was a great ball of fire in the sky. Everyone was alarmed and wondered what was happening. I remember that for hours we could hear ammunition exploding at the impact site.

Later that morning people went to see the wreckage. I was one of them, along with my sister and some of the other villagers. The plane had come to rest nose down on a mountain peak near a large canyon. The force of the impact dropped all four engines into the precipice below. We were able to see some scattered parts but the local authorities and soldiers would not let us get closer to it. How many crew members were recovered, no one seemed to know. There were no survivors. The word was that the plane was on the way to bomb Naples. No one seemed to know just what happened, except that it crashed. Since this occurred at night when everyone was asleep and we saw bombs from the plane scattered about (one even exploded), we concluded that the plane was on the way, rather than returning from a mission. If it was returning from a mission, it would not have bombs left aboard, or that is what we had reasoned.

Upon seeing the bomber wreckage, a fist fight erupted between a fascist and another villager. The fascist argued against Americans bombing Naples and blamed them for all civilian casualties. The other argued against Mussolini and his alliances with Hitler. As a result of the fight, one of them later died of a heart attack. It was kind of freaky. Soon after that a steel cross was erected at the crash site. You could see it from the road -- about a mile or so away. Even today, it is still there. I saw it the last time I was in Italy.

That summer we could see many single engine planes in the skies over the area. They seemed to come so close to us, then climb high and suddenly dive out of our view in order to attack their targets. Besides these, I remember large formations of four engine bombers like a flock of large birds. There were so many you could not count them. The roar of engines was like a swarm of bees, only thousands of times louder. Whether they were B-17 or B-24 bombers, I don't know. They always looked the same to me.

Most young men with their animals would make

their way to the river to water them and catch some shade. At the same time we would swim and bathe. The summers in our area were very hot and dry. It was on one of these days that I remember a large number of bombers traveling over the western mountains in the northwest direction. I do not know where they were headed. As they lumbered northwest there was a scuffle with a small, single engine plane. Just then, one bomber was hit and plummeted down on the mountain, no more than a few miles from where I was standing. There was a large flash of fire and an explosion, but not any secondary explosions. It was surreal but it was becoming common due to the war.

The war was controversial for all of us. It divided the town and caused tensions between people. The dictator Mussolini had his way for a time anyway. As it turned out, by July of 1943, the country of Italy had turned against him and the Grand Council of Fascists jailed him. By September 3, 1943, the nation of Italy signed the Armistice Agreement with the Allies.

I remember my mother sending me to our garden to find some things to use in a tomato salad. I could hear music but did not know where it was coming from. She explained to me that what I was hearing came from our sister village of Latina, less than two miles to our south. They were celebrating the Feast of Our Lady of Graces. That feast is celebrated the weekend closest to September 8. It was on that day that my father, returning from our village, passed by a German armored vehicle. A German uttered, "Traditori Italiani," which means Italian traitors. We knew from that moment on that the Germans were our enemies now. The provisional government tried to keep it secret at first in order to minimize adverse harm from the Germans, but it was too big of a story to keep it secret for long. We were just hoping that the Allies would liberate us and the war would soon come to an end.

I came to understand later the ramifications that followed. After the Armistice, Italy's government was in chaos. The order went out to the Italian military to "put down your arms and save yourselves." It's very easy to say, but much harder to accomplish.

My brother Al made his way home for a time, but was eventually called back to arms against Germany after October 13, 1943. That was when the Italian government was reorganized. It wasn't so easy for my brother Joseph and others stranded in Greece. At that time we didn't know what was going to happen to him. Stranded with no more government to supply them or give them support, our soldiers had to fight against the Germans who were now our enemy. We heard stories that many

Italian soldiers were shot as they made their way back home. Others were captured and taken to prison camps. This was the case with many others in North Africa regions. Some were lucky to be taken by the British and some by Americans too.

We would not hear news about Joseph until the summer of 1945. My mother would sometimes cry privately. I would catch her crying many times. Not knowing if he was alive or fallen was very hard on all of us. We didn't know it but the war was about to hit our area -- up close and personal in a way we were not expecting.

It is my belief that Mussolini had made school attendance mandatory. By age seven, everyone had to be enrolled in school. This must have been the reason I went to school in early October. My seventh birthday was on the fourth. I cannot be sure of the exact date I started but it was the week of my birthday; that much I know for sure. I remember a large classroom. Maybe thirty or forty kids were there in all. I was handed a sheet of lined paper and instructed to write between the lines only. We were told to make all number ones. When I went home, I was showing off my accomplishment. My mother thought they looked like hooks.

The next day, I went to school in a bit of a drizzle. An older boy I knew, whose name was

Gabriel, was standing under the rain spout outside. I knew him because he was my sister's age and lived in town near Uncle Lou and Aunt Mena. Puzzled, I asked him why he was getting wet. He promptly responded that he was "playing wet mouse." I gathered that he wanted to get wet so he could go home instead of staying in school. He noted that I was late for school and if I went upstairs to class, I would get a swat with a ruler in my open hand. I believed him. He was older and I thought he was a "cool cat" from town. So I turned for home. As it turned out, it was a good thing that I did not go to school that day.

I was about halfway home and I could see my father walking toward me. Somehow I was not afraid. I was puzzled more than afraid. As I got closer to him, he beckoned to me to hurry. When I got close he gave me the news. The war front was coming. The Germans were retreating to the north. We needed to get our animals and make a run for the mountains and the countryside.

I had heard that the Germans had orders to live off the land. That meant that fresh meat from our animals, along with our other belongings, was tempting to the German soldiers. We knew they were coming for our food, belongings, and our homes. We had to hide in the mountains for safety.

We later learned that the Germans looted art work. Gold was another prominent item they took. My father found a cavity in one of our walls and hid all our family's gold and sealed it with mortar. Somehow they found it and took it. All of my mother's supplies, including the most difficult ones to find, were also discovered and used or destroyed. They used our wine. They boiled or heated it and put my mother's stash of sugar in it and drank it. My father found this all out later when we returned to our home.

My brother Elio and I took our sheep to a farm outside the village. It was about two miles to the north along the foothill of the mountain. It was a large stone farm built like a fortress. The family that ran the farm was rather large; maybe six to eight children. At one time it must have been owned by an influential person, a doctor or even a baron. There was a large acreage that went with the farm.

Elio had to go back to help my father salvage what they could. The family at the farm asked me to join them at the supper table. Even though I was famished, I was very bashful. I was afraid to do something stupid and embarrassing.

This family at the farm was mostly made up of nice young adult males and three to four girls. The youngest boy who seemed to be about five to six years older than myself was Paolo. The youngest girl was maybe fifteen. The oldest girl was the most attractive. Her name was Rosalina. She was very sweet to me. I would accompany her in some large fields where she would take a large flock of turkeys. I know she had a crush on my brother Al. She also had a smile that could melt an iceberg. I had wished, secretly, that Al would like her, just to have her around. While I eventually would come to America, she married and immigrated to Australia. I actually ran into her one more time when we were both visiting our hometown about thirty years or so later. She gave me a big hug. I was happy to see her. She was just as happy to see me. I still think of her sometimes. It's funny how our paths crossed again all those years later.

After I ate supper they turned in early. I slept next to Paolo and a couple of other brothers in a large bed. The next morning I remember only that Paolo and I took our sheep to graze up the mountains. Apparently my mother had left some homemade bread for me. However, overnight it disappeared. The mother of the house was very apologetic about it. She packed extra bread in Paolo's knapsack with homemade cheese. Later, when we were hungry, I tasted their bread but it contained no salt. The salty cheese helped some but it tasted like nothing I had tasted before -- it was so bland. That was the last thing I needed to worry about. The refugees did not have bread at all.

Refugees would flock in from Naples and other bombed out cities. Some had only what they could carry. Others only had the clothing on their backs. They would have to settle for barns and stables. I had never seen so many people on the move. Now it began to make sense, all the waves of bombers that we used to see. As cities were bombed, refugees would flee. The adults and older boys would caution us younger ones when there was danger of bombs or bullets to lay low or flat, or on our bellies.

The following day, as we were making our way up the mountain, the Americans were dropping bombs on the same mountain only a half mile or so south toward the town. Apparently, they were targeting the German positions. I was temporarily separated from the others. As I attempted to follow their advice to lie flat, I sustained a concussion from the bombings reverberating off of the mountain. It was so strong that it knocked the breath out of my lungs. My stomach felt as though someone gave me an elbow into my gut. The terrain was steep so I began to slide down the mountain. I reached out my hands for anything to stop my fall. I was scared but couldn't even cry. I was too busy trying to stop the downward slide. Luckily, the bombing stopped soon and I was able to find some small bushes that stopped my fall. Then, I went looking for the others. This was my first close call of the war. I'll never forget it.

As we made our way to the crest of the mountain, where we could see both sides, the Germans were passing on the road below us. As we huddled behind rocks we observed them proceed to a large locust grove where they had set up an anti-aircraft battery. There were other gun emplacements too.

When the Americans made their daily visits with small squadrons of about five or six planes -- single engine fight bombers -- they would soar to a steep angle until their motors seemed to almost stall. Then you could hear the roar of engines come back to life at a loud pitch and the fight was on. Gunfire blazed from the planes to the Germans below. The Germans then fired back with A-A batteries. We, of course, rooted for the Americans. It was fun to see such battles. We had the best view from a safe distance away.

Living in the mountains, the war began to wear us down; our supplies began to wane. Our parents would go to our homes and fields in search of food items. Salt was as scarce as sugar by that point.

That explained the bread that Paolo's mother made without salt.

My mother and father were on one of those excursions when the Americans came back. We could see the heavy bombardment that took place. Thick stacks of black smoke filled the sky. One of our churches was flattened. From our view the part of town that was on the slopes was hard to see. We would see later the bomb craters of that day's bombing. It was very emotional. I wondered if I would see my mother again and my father too. I cried uncontrollably. The older boys and my brother Elio would comfort me. It was only by nightfall that my mother came back and I was at peace again. My dad may have been with her; I cannot remember for sure. They were staying with my father's cousin, one half mile farther north. Elio and Al also stayed there. Usually I would run into my family going up the mountain. My sister I would later see when I moved to the farm.

My father had made a couple of trips home to get food for us until the Nazis shot at him with a machine gun. He had to escape through a drainage ditch. Where we were staying, we didn't see the Nazis very much. Only a couple of them showed up at the farm. Armed with a small automatic weapon, they looked around and left. From that point on, they left the farm alone. I guess they didn't want to stray too far from the village.

We did hear of horror stories from others in the community. The Nazis would force the villagers to dig gun emplacements and then shoot them afterward. In another incident, in our sister village of Latina, while a German soldier was getting a shave and a haircut, a local villager motioned to the barber to slit his throat with his razor. When the German soldier was finished with his shave and haircut, he pulled out his pistol, led that man outside where he shot him and threw his body into a well. Apparently, he must have noticed the villager make the motion to slit his throat in the mirror.

Across the river were about a dozen or more farms. They were on the east side of the river. They were beautiful farms, well-built and new looking. They belonged to a company that dealt with wholesale food products. Suddenly one day, we saw them on fire. The Nazis apparently filled them with straw and set them on fire. We could see flames lapping the tops and sides of windows and doors. It must have been in the final days before they would retreat north from our area. I can still remember watching those farms burn. It was tragic. All that beauty and hard work by those farmers was destroyed.

It was late afternoon on this one day when we heard American planes roaring overhead. We looked to our south and saw a convoy of Nazis about one half mile or less in length. As it was moving toward us to the north, the Americans dove over the middle of the line and began strafing it. One of the vehicles was hit. Everything came to a sudden stop. The road was not that wide so they could not have gone around it unless they were driving more carefully and much slower. The damaged vehicle got pushed off the road by another one. The line began to move north again. What I was witnessing was the beginning of our liberation by the Americans. I didn't understand that then but I do now.

On another day, there was a small group of Nazis moving through the mountain. I was not there that day. They came across a party of villagers including my brothers Elio and Al with their animals. This was unusual for the Nazis. Moving in small groups through the forest was not the norm for them. We had never experienced that. They may have been some remnant group, maybe a rear guard of some sort. They were most likely afraid to travel on open spaces and open roads. They asked my brother Al to go fetch them some water. Of course, he complied. He was naturally concerned for the other villagers' safety. They could have been harmed had he not returned.

I am glad that at the time Al was with the Nazis carrying the water, I didn't know it or I would have been worried. There were instances where the Nazis had ordered civilians to do things for them and then would shoot them afterwards. After Al returned from having the Nazis make him accompany them for a few miles, they gave him cigarettes and thanked him and let him go. Some of the German soldiers were polite and respectful. Not every one of them was a tyrant.

Not long after Al had carried water for those German soldiers who were polite to him, things got very quiet. The Germans had simply disappeared. They had made the retreat to the north complete. We found a large Jeep-like vehicle that had been damaged. The camouflage was visibly German. As they made their way north in a hurry, the vehicle was apparently damaged by a land mine. When the vehicle came to a four-way crossing on a country road, there was an apparent land mine explosion. The vehicle must have gone up in the air about twenty feet. There were no survivors.

The Germans were laying land mines as they moved north. This one vehicle must have been hit by those mines. It was one of the last German vehicles we would see. The Americans began to take over from that point on. It was just in time too.

I am not sure how much longer we could have held on with our food and supplies getting so low.

A day or so later, toward the late afternoon, the Americans started shelling the countryside with heavy artillery. As it got later, the roar of cannons became deafening. We moved closer to the foothill of the mountain. It was getting dark by then. Someone got some straw from a nearby farm and they asked me to lie on the straw. I must have fallen asleep. That was the last thing I remember. Next morning I woke up in another bomb shelter near my father's cousin's farm. After looking around I found my sister with me. All the adults were nowhere to be found. There was a heavy fog which made it hard for us to see in front of us. Suddenly, some adults showed up. They told us that the Americans were coming. We were happy to hear the good news, but we were not out of the woods yet.

My parents, along with my sister and me, made our way back toward our village. My brothers were now in charge of our animals. I don't know if they stayed behind at the farms or moved south. As we entered the village on the cobblestone road, we saw a column of American tanks. One tank commander with his hatch open was talking to a local school teacher in French. They both apparently knew the language. Villagers were out on the streets waving and cheering the Americans. Some would throw a candy bar or a piece of chocolate to the kids. The mood was festive and we were relieved. Even though people had suffered destruction from the bombs, there was an aura of optimism and hope.

As the Americans moved north, we on the other hand, moved south. My sister must have stayed with Uncle Lou and Zia Mena because I do not remember her with us when we reached our farm on the Provincial Road, located outside of the village.

As we made our way along to the farm, we could see debris and rubble everywhere. While my parents looked around for food, I was outside playing with some helmets left by the Germans. I had learned that you could fashion a crane from an old umbrella frame. This is what I was doing when a long column of Americans was marching north toward the village. They were in two lines, one on each side of the road. As I hoisted these helmets with my crane, I got the idea to offer them to the marching Americans. I saluted them with the only way I knew -- the Nazi hail salute. Some of them gave me some funny looks. I didn't know the difference between German and American helmets, or the salute. I was, in my own naive way, trying to make friends. One American soldier was moving toward me with a fierce look in his eyes and face. Thankfully, another soldier stopped him before he could get to me. I had irked him with my salute. I did not know the difference.

Shortly after this, we found some beans and lit a fire in our fireplace to cook them. We had just finished eating the cooked beans and we found a piece of German bread on the table. It was hard as a rock and almost black in color. It was rye, no doubt. It looked like a brick. Not long after that, I heard incoming artillery shells. One landed about thirty feet from our front yard. My father was standing in the kitchen doorway. He called out to me and told me to run inside. This was a close call. I could have been hit by the artillery and killed. My mother decided instead to huddle behind the stone wall around the well near the front which was close to the road. I could see debris raining down after being sent up from the explosion. I made it inside without a scratch but my mother was not so lucky. A large chunk of dirt hit her on the lower back. For a moment I thought this was it for her. She laid there for a while in excruciating pain, but eventually was able to get up and walk.

Inadvertently, we invited trouble when we lit a fire in our fireplace to cook the beans. The smoke out of the chimney must have made the Germans, now miles away, suspicious. They launched their artillery shells at us and almost killed us.

We made our way south along the Provincial Road. Luckily the Americans had already cleared it for land mines. We met no one along the two mile stretch. We made our way to a farm in Latina. The farm was swarmed with people. It looked like a beehive. It was twilight and we were shown to a large barn. The floor was full of straw all along its wall sides. I must have been tired and quickly fell asleep because I don't remember anything else until the next morning. To my surprise I ran into my friend Josephine. She and her mother were there also. There were Americans nearby as well. There was a field with reconnaissance planes. We had seen these fly overhead but never close up. I always wondered why the Germans never took any shots at these low flying planes. Somehow I found out that they didn't want to give away their positions. Since they were unarmed and of little value to shoot down, they didn't bother.

Josephine and I made our way exploring and wanting to see these stork-like planes up close and personal -- that is until some Americans made it clear not to get any closer. As we left the improvised air field, we followed a country lane to the farm. We could tell that Americans had camped there overnight. There were empty instant coffee cans, candy wrappers, and other things that suggested their stay. As we got closer to the farm, we realized our parents were furious we went without permission. They had been looking for us. Only our mothers were still there. Our fathers must have left early to meet up with other members of our families. They were still a few miles from where we lodged the night before, taking care of our animals. We were just being curious kids.

By now, everyone was going their own way. As my mother and I made our way back toward Baia looking for my brothers and father, we came upon an American company of infantry. There was no other soul on that road. When they came within our view, you would have thought they saw a ghost. I think they were surprised to see a woman and young boy alone, walking toward a deserted town. We were on our way to another farm house about two miles away.

As we got closer to the company of soldiers, we could see they were eating their rations. My mother, probably ashamed to ask them for any food, motioned to them that I was hungry. I was even more ashamed. I pretended that I was not hungry.

I had not eaten since the day before at our farm when we were sent running from the Germans shelling us. I was afraid, perhaps needlessly, that I would take from them the only food they had on hand. I didn't feel right. Had they offered us some from their backpacks, I might have taken some because then I would have known that they had more food on hand.

As we made our way off the Provincial Road we took some country roads. One such road was narrow and was marked with what appeared to be land mine warning signs. We had heard that road was mined. A close family friend had taken that same road going to a grain mill in the next town. Walking behind a donkey laden with a sack of wheat, he barely escaped with his life when a mine exploded. I felt bad for the donkey who was hit. We were afraid to walk on that road, but we had no other way to get where we wanted to go. We took our chances and walked the road.

Someone we met on our way, almost to our destination, gave us some meat. A farmer's cow had been killed by a bomb or artillery shell. I can't remember who it was that gave us the meat. It was plainly boiled with no salt. It wasn't the best I had ever tasted. However, when you are hungry, you make do with what you have. I ate just enough to satisfy my hunger.

These were very tough times for us as you can imagine. We didn't know where our next meal would come from. We wanted to ask the Americans for some food but felt ashamed doing so. Even though we were prepared to deal with the hunger pains, it was sure nice to finally come upon some boiled meat. We had to make due with whatever meager food we could scrape up.

My family was not poor before the war. We may not have been rich either, but we were self-sufficient and lived a good middle-class life. Having to scrounge for food and beg the Americans for a meal was very humiliating. I guess when you have to survive you do what it takes to save your life and the lives of your family. It makes you appreciate the value of life.

Chapter 3: Picking Up the Pieces

We were lucky to have survived all of the violence. Our town endured extensive damage from the bombing campaign. Many people lost their homes. It would be a long time, in some cases two to three years, before rebuilding could even begin for some people.

When surveying our farm we noticed that some damage was done, but at least it was repairable. We were lucky that we at least could move back into our home. Some others were not so lucky. Our roof needed some terra cotta channel tiles. They were eventually replaced. All of our rooms were full of dust and debris. The front of the farm had an artillery shell stuck in the eaves. Luckily it did not explode. My brother Al theorized that the projectile was an armor piercing type. Being that the eave was softer than armor, it didn't explode. The shell was removed very gently. What happened to it, I can't remember. Come to think of it, there was a lot of ordnance lying around. Eventually, sometime later, it was gathered and taken away. Some young men that weren't careful lost their lives when tinkering with them. Others lost limbs trying to disarm them. It seemed like the tragedies of war continued long after the battles were over.

As we moved back to our farm and embraced some sense of normalcy, we worried about our brother Joe. We made repeated attempts to find news about him through the Red Cross, but never found out anything. We would hear horror stories about how some soldiers froze to death on the Eastern Front. Others were stranded in the deserts of North Africa where some died of hunger and thirst. Could one of them have been Joe? The fear of the unknown was overwhelming at times.

Within days, the Americans were moving in our areas and in greater numbers. Everywhere in the countryside huge camps were established. The earlier wave of Americans had moved on toward Cassino. There, the Germans were fortified inside the mountain, armed with huge guns. They were successful in holding the allies off for months. After they settled in and artillery pieces were dug into their positions, they rested for a time. Then they launched offensives for Cassino one after another. In the beginning we would see German planes make their daily run over the camps. One half-track armored car was in our vineyard for camouflage. As the Americans were talking to my father and me, the planes made their run. The Americans motioned for us to get away from there. It would have been dangerous for us to hang around.

On another day, as I was watching my sheep in a field nearby, the planes made a comeback. Being young and naive, I was watching the fight as a spectator, not realizing that I could be in danger during the crossfire until my father called out for me to take cover. I felt that they could see that I was not a threat. I wanted to watch the flack of anti-aircraft batteries with wonder as the German planes swarmed above the Americans, not realizing that I could have been killed.

As I moved about the fields on another day, just at the foot of the mountain, there was a tank parked nearby. The crew must have been resting. One of them seemed glad to see me. This location was just below where the four engine plane had crashed in spring time. He was asking me about the crater nearby and how it happened. He spoke Italian. Our conversation was cut short by German planes. He told me to get away quickly for fear of any harm to me. So my sheep watching chores were good for me. I got to go to the mountains and countryside. I knew where there were ammunitions and where the American soldiers would go for firing ranges. I made friends with the American soldiers and even got a treat of candy on some occasions. I was like a freelance observer at seven years of age.

Eventually the Germans stopped coming our way. Everything became so much quieter. Some of the American officers had taken a room at our farm. They enjoyed talking with my father, whose English was not fluent, but he could carry on a conversation. Many times my mother would give them homemade food. They raved about it. Of course, she did it wholeheartedly, hoping that maybe another mother somewhere might do the same thing for my brother Joe.

The American troops that we made friends with would return from Cassino for R&R since Cassino was not liberated until late May of 1944. The American troops made more than one foray for Cassino. When they came back, they would come to see us. They even brought us nice pieces of furniture once.

I wish I would have known that someday I would come to America; then I would have taken down their names and addresses. It would have been great to have thanked them for liberating us. It would have been even more amazing if I could have developed a friendship with some of them.

I will always remember the patch on their uniforms. It had blue stripes on white. Many years later I would come to know that this was the unit patch for the US Army's 3rd Infantry Division.

One American soldier named Frank would come by our place in the mornings. He would bring news to the camp which was just a quarter mile from our farm. He liked to come to our stable and say, "Good morning Mr. Jack Ass and Mr. Donkey." We thought that it was funny.

The Americans spent much of the winter of 1943-1944 with us. By spring of 1944 they made their move closer to Cassino where they took part in the battle of Monte Cassino.

During the wet and muddy winter we could hear the bombardment of Cassino on an almost nightly basis. I estimate the distance was twenty-five to thirty miles away from our farm.

We had a door to the back room of our house and every time the bombardments took place, the door would rattle on its hinges. The ground would shake as if an earthquake was upon us. I pitied the poor soldiers who were up close on the front lines. That must have been hell for them.

That winter and in the spring of 1944, I was able to move about our property and go farther with my sheep. I was able to get up on the mountains as well as in the countryside. So I visited the northern parts where we had been hiding from the Nazis until the Americans came. I could tell that after we moved south, when the Americans had first arrived, there must have been some fierce battles in the days afterward. I discovered two burned out American tanks. I didn't get to explore one of them. The other one I was able to enter. The interior was partially burned. There were ammunitions that had exploded inside. At first I was curious about it all. The fire inside must have been extinguished. Among fragments of ammunitions, there was a puddle of what seemed to be fuel oil. Had the fire not been put out, the fuel oil would have been consumed. I ran out of the tank when I discovered what seemed to be human bone remains, possibly an arm bone.

Another time I was playing with a bone. I thought it was an animal bone. When someone told me that it could be human, I dropped it and washed my hands multiple times.

In another field about two miles south, a German tank was abandoned. It had a broken track. It seemed otherwise in good shape. Some kids figured out how to get inside and rotate the gun turret. As one would hold the button, others rode the gun barrel as a merry go round. That was until someone removed the battery. With that battery and a small generator, we were able to have power for our first festival after the front had passed on. All of our power lines were cut after Cassino was liberated late that spring of 1944. The Americans and some British moved on from our area. What we saw more of from that time forward were Canadians and Scots. After a brief period they too moved on.

The summer of 1944 became a real quiet time for us. I continued my sheep watching job. It would be about two more years before schools opened. I forgot all about school by that point. I continued my exploits up on the mountains as well as in the countryside.

Being a shepherd was a double edged sword. At times it could be fun; other times it was quite lonely. I had to find ways to entertain myself. Because of the nature of grass and where and when it was available, we shepherds moved about almost like nomads for greener pastures. We used the mountains mostly in winter. By late fall we returned to the mountains.

During the fall the countryside was seeded for crops. The roads were in those times more muddy. At times, I would direct my sheep toward a mountain top. After a few hours I would turn them back toward the point of origin and then eventually home. I could either follow them or walk on the road below until it was time to head them back. I encountered other boys on the road. We would get together and engage in different games and fun. These were the good times. If we met other boys on the mountains we were happy for the encounters. It made the time more fun and helped it to pass quickly. The more boys, the more fun we could have. On days when we chose other zones for greener grass and did not meet other company, it could be boring and depressing.

By spring, the mountains would rejuvenate themselves with lush grasses. The wild flowers were magical and they were as unique as they were beautiful. But even that magic would only last for a season. As May approached, the dry weather would follow. The grass would turn brown. The wild shrubs and their flowers would continue their glory. They were more deeply rooted than grass. In turn, we made for the countryside where grass was now high and greener. Unlike the mountains where the soil was very thin, the country roadsides and some fields were fertile with good soil. After harvesting was complete, more fields would become available for use as pastures.

In our area and latitude, spring sometimes would come early. This was exciting for us as shepherds. When spring came the sap would start to flow under the bark of trees. There is a way of removing a length of bark intact and making whistles from it. Sometimes by March we could begin making whistles from certain types of trees. Willow was one such tree. Poplar was another. It seems like nothing now, but to us it was a huge pastime. Through the summer we braided sling shots from the fiber of cannabis plants (hemp). When my father told me that in America they smoked the leaves I thought that they were crazy because it smelled so bad.

In the fall we made spinning tops and sometimes we made whistles from cane plants. It was another way to pass the time.

The summers were extremely hot and dry. We didn't get rain for long periods of time. When a flock of sheep would walk the dusty dry roads, they lifted a cloud of dust behind them. Somehow they tend to drag their hind hooves. I usually walked far behind on their flanks. During these hot and dry periods we mostly hung around the river side. There was more greenery as well as water for our animals. We of course went swimming too, in spite of our parents' warnings. There were treacherous areas of the river. An occasional drowning would happen at times. One area in particular was known for deep whirlpools and many different drownings. Legends abounded about how deep some parts were. According to some villagers, they could not find the depths of that area. Some swimmers would dive off the banks and never surface again. I avoided that area like the plague.

On one occasion while walking across an area of the river with a friend, I fell into the water and went off into the deep end. I had lost my balance and down I went. For a short time, I even lost consciousness. Luckily, someone pulled me out. I was more embarrassed than I was scared. From that time going forward, I made myself a promise that I would learn to swim, even if I drowned trying. I never told my parents about it. Eventually, I would learn to swim on my own. I chose safe areas until I had enough confidence for the deep.

As fall would come, it seemed like another spring had arrived. After a rain in late August or so, everything would turn green again. It seemed even greener than spring itself. The country roadsides, the fields and even the mountains were lush again. There seemed to be green everywhere you could look. The temperature was a bit higher than early spring. It all would last until late October and even into November when the rainy season usually came. By then it was time for me to head back to the mountainsides.

Finding green grass was very rewarding for the sheep. I felt like a mother might feel when a child ate well and was satisfied. It was the same when my charge, my sheep, had plenty of grass and the sides of their bellies rounded out. What was also rewarding was finding new watering holes, sometimes even a new discovery of a rock formation, or a new pathway to a green valley. Other times while exploring with a friend or two, I explored canyons and hidden water sources -- miles from the nearest well.

Sheep would give birth in fall and again in spring. These were happy times too. There is nothing more pleasing than holding a new baby lamb in your arms. Sometimes the mother would get jealous and you got head butted, but usually they were accommodating. It was a beautiful feeling to bring a new lamb into the world. My father taught me how to help a mother during birth -- and then clear away any mucus from the lamb's mouth and nose area so it would breathe normally. The mother would eventually clean the whole lamb. It would become white as snow. Usually, it takes a few hours until the new lamb can walk long distances. I would put it in my arms as I made my way home. I was happy to carry it while the mother followed me. My brother Elio would tease me. He would say that I licked the lamb's nose. I knew that he was only teasing, but I would get really mad about it. In short, you become attached to your animals. The bad thing about animals is that you must be able to be there for them, even when you don't want to be. At times I would miss various events in town because the sheep needed my care.

I will always remember the story of Nicolotto. Nicolotto was the name I gave to a lamb. He was by nature an unlucky lamb from the start. When his mother gave birth, she was a first time mother. She would not have anything to do with the lamb. It would make me mad that he needed to suckle milk from his mother and she would not let him. I would hold her neck between my legs and I would put him in position so he could have his fill of milk. In time he became attached to me. He would hang around me instead of his mother. He did eventually join the company of other sheep.

One day, as I was taking the flock to pasture I was traveling along the main road to one side. A certain individual by the nickname of Nicolotto happened to pass by on his bike. Somehow the lamb got too close to the bike and his hind leg got caught in the bike's spokes.

The leg was broken. We fashioned a splint and cast for it. This is how the lamb got his name, Nicolotto.

I felt so sorry for him. That was only the beginning of his fate. As he grew a bit more, on one occasion, there was a flood in town. The stable of a villager got flooded. This man asked if he could house his sheep with ours -- in our stable overnight. My father of course agreed, although we were limited with space already. Next morning, when I was ready to take the sheep to pasture, we found poor Nicolotto trampled to death. I felt so bad. I might have even cried. There were tender moments like these that I still remember. Nicolotto is just one of them. Those tender moments made it worth missing the fun activities that went on in town during the day time.

People did not seem to have much regard for shepherds. It was kind of a menial job but I grew to enjoy it because of the attachment to the sheep. There is much more to it than just watching sheep eat grass. You must also care for them in regard to their health. For one thing, in the summer months they would get many ticks inside of their ears. The ticks would inflate with the sheep's blood and I would carefully remove them and crush them. Sometimes their hooves would get a fungus and there was a need to trim their hooves and treat their wounds with what, I think, is called copper oxide. Then we would bind them and give them a chance to heal properly. You had to protect them from wolves or other predators. For the most part, wolves were scarce in our area but you always had to be on guard, just in case.

The shepherds who would come down to our area for the winter were from a higher mountain elevation. Their dogs had collars with spikes on them. This prevented the wolves from killing the dogs that watched their flocks. These were real professional shepherds. They made a living from it. For us, it was a side job. The income from the sale of the lambs and their wool was nice though. It also meant that we had lamb to eat for Easter and Christmas. We would cook it in a brick oven. Roasted lamb from a brick oven, with potatoes, was always delicious.

Chapter 4: 1945, A Year Like No Other

1945 was a year to like no other. First the Germans surrendered. Then some news about my brother Joe surfaced. Somehow, Al found out that our brother Joe was in Lubeck, a German prison camp. I was so stunned at first that I did not want to believe it. He often was a teaser and made up tall tales. After a while, I was convinced that it could actually be true.

My mind began racing as I thought about Joe. I was always elated when my brothers came home on leave from the service. I was so proud of them. They were my heroes. Now, I could not wait for Joseph to come home to us. I had not seen him for years. I wondered what he would look like.

One day, a person notified us in advance that Joe was on his way home from the train station. He sent word so that we would not be shocked. We ran on foot to meet him. He had gotten a ride on a horse driven cart. When we got to him, he dismounted and we all embraced and cried with joy. We walked the rest of the way home. As we walked, we talked and got used to each other again. He was now a stocky man, dressed in civilian clothes and close to six feet tall. He seemed like a giant to me.

It was hard to imagine that a short time earlier he was skin and bones and I was about to be nine years old. I am sure that I had not seen him for at least four years, or close to it. He asked, "Is this Dom?" I guess he was also surprised that I had grown.

By the time we got home, our kitchen was full of people -- neighbors, friends and relatives. There was so much joy and celebrating that it went on for a long time. Suddenly, Joseph left the crowded room. He went into our pantry and was crying out loud like a baby. We didn't know at that moment why he was crying at a happy homecoming. He then replied that he was crying for all his friends who did not make it home. As he recalled stories of the prison camp, things became more somber. The conditions of the prison camp were terrible. One story in particular always chokes me up when I think of it. Joe spoke of how the prisoners received only one small piece of bread to eat every other day. Often the prisoners would look for other things to eat as they were taken on work details or work farms. They would scrounge for potato skins, orange skins, or anything they could get their hands on without being seen.

One day in their camp, they received their meager bread allotment. One prisoner bent down to pluck a leaf of what looked like a dandelion. It was forbidden for the prisoners to stoop down. A German guard fired his rifle over the head of the prisoner to warn him. Just then, the prisoner stood up! The bullet struck him between the eyes. It was such a sad scene, even the German guard cried.

This story proved to me that there were Germans who did have a conscience, just like the ones who spent time with Alfonso when he fetched water for them. They made him carry the water for a few miles, but then they gave him cigarettes and let him go. We seem to think of only the bad ones. There are always a few good souls in the crowd. It was just hard to know who they were as the Nazis were so ruthless. The Nazis may have given the German people a bad name, but that is totally unfair to the German people. You can hardly hold the entire German people responsible for the actions of the Nazi Party.

Joe told us of a time when he helped a fellow prisoner who was having trouble with his chores. The Germans beat Joe mercilessly because he helped the other prisoner. There were other horrible stories that were too numerous to count. They made us appreciate the fact that Joe was finally home. With my brother Joe home, my family was now complete. Things began to make sense again. I now had the chance to put the past behind me. I could start remembering the good old days and start making new memories to replace the old ones.

By the following year, the local school began to offer classes again. Since the time I had attended just two days of school in 1943, before the Nazis took over our town, I had experienced just brief periods of time where I was able to learn some basics in writing and reading. My parents had sent me to a couple of different places to learn but it was short lived due to the war. These were, for me, a waste of time. The people that taught me were either lazy or unprofessional. That just made me more apprehensive toward learning.

When the school year of 1946-1947 began, I was almost ten years old. As I and another boy were watching our sheep, he asked me if I could watch his sheep for three to four hours because he was going to public school. He was a bit younger than me so I felt a surge of resentment -- not against the boy, but against my parents. Here was a boy from a family whose means were no greater than my family's, yet he was getting an education while I was not. I went home that day and demanded to go to school. To my surprise, my parents agreed. So I started going to school too. My time spent with my sheep taught me a lot, but now, I was ready and hungry for real knowledge.

Because the war had delayed my education by about three years, there were younger children in my first grade class. But there were others who were also in my situation. I welcomed my school and the opportunity to learn. I was ripe and hungry for learning. What impressed me the most was one of the most basic things -- the alphabet. I discovered that each letter was a building block. This is what the other amateur teachers did not present to me. Finally, I was arming myself with the building blocks of knowledge. I also learned basic mathematics. It was the subject I loved the most. Numbers seemed to open for me a new horizon. I was finally on my way.

When I started second grade I was introduced to what would become a great teacher. He insisted that we call him "Professor." One young man, for some reason, would always call him "Maestro," which means "Teacher," -- that used to infuriate him. I don't know why he would get so infuriated. Whether he had the credentials of a professor I don't know. I called him "Professor" and that was ok with the both of us. This man could teach very effectively. He had a way of putting ideas and concepts into a short sentence that he uttered to us and it stuck to our minds like a magnet. It did for some anyway. He seemed straight laced and of few words but he didn't miss a trick. It was in his class during second grade that we learned all the math operations. When it came to learning and knowing our multiplication tables by heart, we would compete with each other for the best of the class. We attended school for about four hours per day, six days per week. We had to share classes with other children because there was not enough room in the building for more students. Thankfully for me, I was able to skip the third grade and go right to fourth grade.

One day in early June or late May, my family was working a tract of land by the river, about two miles from the school. Becoming so occupied by the work there, I almost forgot about school. The large clock on the municipal building would ring every fifteen minutes. Being located at a high point, it would carry the sound for a great distance. When I heard its ring, it reminded me that on this day we had a multiplication (times table) contest. I was almost praying that it was not too late and that I would make it in time for school. My big brother Joe said, "Take my bike and you can still make class." I got on that bike and pedaled as fast as possible to make my class in time. I arrived with no time to spare. They had already started the contest for multiplication tables. Professor Fusco told me that I had to go against the best kid in the class. I guessed it had something to do with my being late.

As we were asked the multiplication tables, the top contestant and I came to a stalemate. Then, Professor Fusco sent us upstairs to be asked questions by the fifth grade teacher. After some time, neither of us would yield. Ultimately, we became co-champs of multiplication tables.

I met Professor Fusco going up to my fourth grade class one day. When they let me skip from third grade to fourth, he said to me, "I told your fourth grade teacher that you were top gun." I never knew that he thought that about me. I just froze. But it felt good that someone noticed and appreciated my efforts. I still remember the way that he taught us all the prepositions in the Italian language by using only four words. It was a mnemonic device of sorts. I also learned a more efficient way to do math.

Some years later, when in America, I helped one of my colleagues with his math homework using these same techniques. The following day when the teacher saw the work, the teacher asked that student who had taught them to do math this way. They called it "modern math." Wow, modern math. This professor had taught me this math around 1948 when I was in the second grade. So he was onto something when he wanted to be called "Professor." I never can forget him. He inspired me to learn more and learn in a better way. I am amazed that while we didn't have any fancy schools or even long days in class, these teachers really tried to do the best for us to help us get on with life right after the war.

By now I was becoming a more knowledgeable shepherd for my age. I came home one evening and I saw a wicker basket full of dried fruits. They must have been dried at the peak of maturity. The figs had on them a coating that seemed like frost. It was just a natural sugar from the figs themselves. There were also pears, peaches, and maybe plums. It was all a super delicious mixture of fruits. I asked my mother about all the goodies and she explained that there was a boy just about a year or two younger than myself. His name was Lorenzo. His father bought him some sheep. He needed a mentor or a guide because he knew nothing about sheep. I was volunteered by my parents to be the mentor for Lorenzo. The large basket of dried fruit was the offering for the favor. I took Lorenzo on and we became very tight friends. I remember that he was very shy. He and his family lived just a quarter mile from my house. There were other boys that lived in that same group of homes. They seemed somewhat backward.

As it turned out Lorenzo came to call me every morning when it was time to bring our sheep to pasture. He would whistle from behind some hedges until I heard him. Then we would meet and walk together.

As time went on I started to find out a few things about him. Apparently he had already experimented with tobacco. His father right after the war bought tobacco leaves and rolled his own cigarettes. What follows, of course, is so predictable. We both started rolling cigarettes. With his father's supply we steadily rolled and puffed. Sometimes we were short on matches or paper to roll our own cigarettes. His brother and cousins picked up on what was happening and they would squeal on us. So we developed a code word system for each item that we obtained. This way, before he left the house, he knew what we didn't have and tried to get it before we left. But his brother and cousins were like watch dogs and kept guard over all we did and said.

One evening we were close to our homes with our sheep. We thought we would have a last cigarette. We were so sure that we were safe and we didn't try to hide it. As we were puffing away, his father returned from work riding on a donkey. All of a sudden we heard him say, "Oh, you smoke?" What was funny was that he said it in English. We were so surprised that we froze. We never expected him to take this road. It was more of a lane than a road because it was somewhat narrow and very seldom used. But he nailed us. I think Lorenzo got a few swats on the butt that night.

Other boys would ask us for some and we made them do chores for us. We would tell them to go fetch our sheep when they were going places other than where we expected them to go. One day I told Lorenzo not to give so much tobacco away as we might just run out. He responded that his one pocket contained pure tobacco for us and the other contained filler leaves of various plants. I was surprised. He was a bit shy and somewhat backward, but he knew how to stretch tobacco with other leaves of maybe potatoes and other plants.

Lorenzo and I had become so close when we watched sheep together and sometimes we would have spats. He told me one day, "Don't come for me tomorrow. I don't want to go with you anymore." I did as he said. Next morning I went to the mountains alone. I learned later that he would not take his sheep out that day. He brought them near his home somewhere and would break branches of trees and fed the leaves to his sheep. The next morning I went by his house to get him. He told me, "Don't pay attention to me if ever I say not to come for me." I never figured out what the problem was so

I let it go.

Another thing that he and I would do was to play near a creek that ran near his home. During the spring, frogs and/or what we thought were toads would lay eggs in the shallow part of the creek. They laid long lines of transparent strings with dotted black eggs every fourth of an inch or less. We were fascinated by them. Eventually the eggs would morph into tadpoles. There were so many of them. We couldn't believe how many eggs one of these small creatures could lay. They just moved ever so slow but it seemed a never-ending process. Later on we would notice that all the tadpoles would move to deeper water. Later we noticed how each tadpole would become small frogs. Some were greener than others. We thought if they were green they would become frogs and the darker colored ones would become toads. Lorenzo could not stomach the toads. They were ugly and people used to say that they could spray you with poisonous mist.

One day Lorenzo was looking at all those creatures and he said he didn't want toads to live, only frogs. So he asked me to help him to destroy what we perceived to be toads and let the frogs live. We reasoned that frogs would grow large and we could harvest frog legs. I am glad that we didn't follow through with the idea. That would have been cruel.

For a while we were quite "the two rascals." There were times when we would get some fresh eggs from the farm and bring them to a store in town and get some spending money from them. We now could buy pocket knives and some other trinkets. If our parents would have known we would surely have gotten in trouble.

The other thing I greatly enjoyed was when a group of us young boys and girls would chip in and bring things from home and then we would have a cook out. Once, a young man brought a chicken and told his family that a fox had eaten the chicken. Life could be hard but we did manage to have some fun.

As I started school full time, we didn't see each other as often. Later we ended up selling our sheep and I started my course of study privately. Lorenzo, his brother, and a cousin started going to night school and I don't remember how long he had his sheep after that.

Eventually I came to America and lost touch with Lorenzo and his brother and cousins. It was in the early 1960's that I got to see him. He had married and immigrated to Canada. As my wife and I visited her cousins there, we found out that Lorenzo was in Toronto. We went to see him and reminisced about the times when we had tobacco in our early years in Italy.

Some years later, my wife and I were back in Canada. We were shocked to hear that my friend Lorenzo had contracted cancer of the stomach and had passed on. Once again, I had lost another friend from my hometown. He will always be in my thoughts.

As I moved along with school, the flock of sheep became smaller. Eventually, we sold them all. Soon after that, I moved to cattle care, especially when Elio was drafted into the Italian army for a full year. This was mandatory once you were eighteen. Once again, I had something to look forward to when he came home on leave in his uniform. At least this time, there was no war and we did not have to worry about Elio like we did with Al and Joe.

I was not always proficient in some of my chores. I was not trained in all things because of my sheep duties. There were other boys younger than me that could perform some routine things, such as putting a team of oxen under the yoke and attaching them to a cart. It was on such an occasion that my father, for the first time, ordered me to do so. I had never done it before. When I said that I did not know how to do it in the presence of a neighbor, he retorted that he had the dumbest kids. I was so ashamed and angered that I stopped trying to do it and fled. I was hurt because he should have not expected me to do something that I was never shown. Because an outsider was present, it made me feel bad. It was so humiliating.

As time went on, I learned how to do the things I needed to do. I was now about twelve or thirteen years old. I must have been in the middle of third grade elementary school. It was then that I noticed a young man who couldn't grasp Roman history. One day his father dropped into class and was talking about history being a bit tough for his son. When our teacher called on me to repeat the lesson, I was surprised. Afterward, the father of the young man noted that I was older, which was true. It was due to the war. However, after talking it over with the fourth and fifth grade teacher, I was moved to the fourth grade. This same teacher had both fourth and fifth grades in a large classroom. Now I was learning fourth grade courses and catching some fifth grade lessons as well. In a few months, my fourth grade teacher said I could take exams with a night school class to earn my fifth grade diploma. I was the youngest of that night school class taking the exam. Thanks to my full time schooling, I scored the best of all the kids in the class. I was finally catching up on the time lost during the war.

After getting my fifth grade diploma, my dream was to complete middle school and reach the other students in high school. To do that, I would have to do three years of schooling in one. This would propel me to high school level. Many tried to discourage me. They said it was too hard. I knew others had done it, so I knew it was possible. That gave me hope. Besides, if I didn't pass exams for three grades, maybe I could pass two at least. I started my studies privately to finish three years in one year.

The load was heavy. I would go to a teacher in the afternoon and another in the early mornings. In between, I cared for cattle as well. Sometimes Alfonso would come to relieve me of my duties so I could go to school. I could see that he hated it. Privately he was proud of me. His friends would tell me. He was sort of the cool type. Even his name sounds like the cool guy we know from the series *"Happy Days"* -- Alfonso sounds a lot like "The Fonz." If he could have avoided coming to watch the animals for me, I am sure he would have done it. That's why my father pegged him the "English Lord." Sometimes he would call him, "The Don Ottavius." I never knew exactly what that meant. It was just kind of funny to hear it.

My brother, Alfonso, really hated farm work. He often would come up with schemes and ideas to shorten or avoid doing jobs. He liked modern methods of farming, especially the use of tractors and bulldozers. He would surely have loved America. He was innovative. Often, he proposed to do great things. The trouble was they were often expensive to implement. He did stick to his guns and eventually contracted with a company that brought modern machinery to town. He got to run the bulldozer for plowing land and was happy. He was even planning to marry. Like so many other things that occurred in my family, his dreams were never fulfilled.

Chapter 5: Unfulfilled Dreams

Around 1948, my parents made an attempt to come to America. Since they were both American born, they didn't expect any problems. After a time, they were notified by mail that they had both lost their American citizenship. I guess what happed was that after the chaos of the war, in 1946, there were national elections. There were many parties from which to choose. But hardly anyone knew anything about these new parties. My parents only knew that before Mussolini, the king was fair to all his citizens and therefore they chose to vote for the monarchy. It was their way of rejecting Mussolini's Fascist Party. Unbeknownst to them, the Americans preferred for them to vote for the Christian Democratic Party. Actually, they didn't want to vote at all, for fear of such repercussions. It was the local officials who pressed them to vote. They told my parents to vote using a blank ballot as this was to protect their American citizenship. They were required to vote, so they did. According to the prevailing laws right after the war, that was the rule, even if it was unfair.

What a shame. My parents did not even want to vote. They were forced to do so. As a result, my parents were told they could not immigrate to the nation where they were born. It was just another tragic let down for them. There certainly were a lot of disappointments in my parents' lives. When I think of what they endured, it seems almost too hard to digest. There would be more disappointments and tragedies lying in wait for them after I immigrated to the USA.

My parents were both born in America, in 1895 and 1896, my father being one year older. They were both born in Western Pennsylvania, near the Eastern Ohio border in a small town called Hillsville. They were brought back to Italy as children. Years later, my father returned to America as a young man at eighteen. His hope was to earn some fast money, work in the steel mills of Western Pennsylvania, and send home money to buy farm land. Then maybe he could get married. When he heard about America getting into World War I, he decided to go home thinking he could avoid being drafted. Unfortunately, when he returned to Italy, he was promptly drafted into the Italian Army to fight against the Germans, Austrians, and Albanians. It was just another difficult situation that he had to overcome.

My father took the struggle in stride. He became a cavalryman and was proud of it. He would often speak of fighting in Albania. After the war he met my mother and eventually they were married by the mid-1920's. They shared the same experience of having been born in Hillsville and then brought back to Baia when they were children. My mother always wanted to see where she was born. That is why she and my dad decided to visit America. They had all the papers made and they were ready to embark on their journey. However, it was not to be. Hearing other people from the village talk of the impending hard times caused by the Great Depression, they called off their trip. My father reasoned that they would always eke out a living on their small farm. They never did get rich, but they were self-sufficient.

By the time the Great Depression ended, World War II began. Then, after the war, they were denied entry to the United States again, all because they unwittingly voted and lost their American citizenship. It would seem that things were not in their favor. They were heartbroken. With so much tragedy and so much pain already endured by my parents, how could this be happening now? This seemed like just another one of those tough breaks that had become so common for them.

It was after this news that each of us took our own paths. Elio, after his stint in the Army, chose a career as a Carabiniere -- the national police force. Joe was an agent of sorts for farmers. He would bring customers to them. These were people looking for grain, land, or animals to buy and Joe helped make it possible. He played the part of a mediator. Al liked to contract farmers to have their land plowed by tractor or bulldozer. Bulldozers could plow much deeper than tractors. Many fields after the war were so compressed from military tank traffic that they needed to be plowed deep in order that crops might have a chance to grow. Also, deep plowing promoted deeper roots for the summer crops, especially in dry regions such as ours. In the summer, this provided a huge assistance to the farmers. Al had stumbled upon a good business opportunity.

As I continued to strive for a better education, my parents were urged by my brother Elio to help me continue. Elio was my champion. He always looked out for me. I cannot forget the cold winters growing up and how he made sure I was warm. When we went to bed he would always say, "Put your cold feet near my legs." It was a sense of security and protection that he provided.

I remember when Elio was in his late teens and contracted pneumonia. He had to stay in bed for a period of time. Since both of our bedrooms were upstairs, he would call for me. Other times my parents would send me upstairs to keep him company. He loved that. He would tell me all these funny stories just to keep me there with him.

I looked up to Elio and could not wait to see him when he came home on leave. He looked like a real tough guy when he used to wear his Carabiniere uniform. I was so proud of him. He was also a hard worker. All the people that we exchanged working days with would ask us to send Elio. He left a rather big impression upon me and many others in the community.

Al was more distant with me. He was much older than me and into the good life. He was handsome, witty, and charming. He had a large following among the girls in the community. My father would tease him about his attitude. They sometimes would get into little discussions where they would tease one another in a kidding manner. I used to enjoy the show. The titles my father gave him were so fitting for his behavior.

Joe was more of a quiet and fun loving guy. He would not hurt you if he could help it. He had a "live and let live" attitude. My sister Mena on the other hand always wanted to be my boss and superior. We had many battles. I always thought that I had to keep her from ruling over me. It was typical brother and sister spats.

After the war, things started looking up for the family. Everyone was busy doing their thing. However, it was, as they say, "the calm before the storm."

Because we were located by the main road, we often got strangers and all kinds of sales people at our door, including gypsies. It was on a cool morning that Al and I were talking to my mother and warming ourselves by the fire. We heard a knock at the door. A gypsy lady appeared. She was not trusted by people in the community because of her fascination with the occult. She wanted to tell our fortune in exchange for a piece of lard or bacon. My mother told her to get lost. However, she proceeded to tell my mother that one of her sons would die young and another would make a trip across the ocean. She also stated that there was a curse upon my family. She said that if my mother would give her what she wanted, then she would take away the curse. Mom was so infuriated that she threw her out of the house. Of course, gypsies cannot tell the future any more than I can. It was strange that she got some of the things correct, though not all things. At times I have wondered if what she said was just a coincidence, or if by some freak chance that some of her predictions came true. Whatever the case may be, what happened next was a real punch to the gut.

It was early May of 1952. We had received a letter from Elio. He thought that he had contracted a terrible disease. He spoke of doing harm to himself. We were terrified and shocked. My parents had me go see his girlfriend. I asked if everything was ok between them. She said everything was fine. My brother Al quickly ran to catch a train to Taranto, the location where Elio was stationed in the military. My father too ran for the train the next day.

When Al got to his barracks, the guard on duty said Elio was out on liberty and suggested that Al go and wait for Elio in his dorm room. When Elio returned later that night, the sentry asked Elio if he was Merola. Elio responded, "Why do you ask me that?" The sentry replied, "If you are not Merola, then forget it." He never did tell Elio that Al was waiting for him. Had Elio known that his brother was there waiting for him, a terrible tragedy may have been averted.

Depressed and under the impression that he was going to suffer, Elio proceeded to walk into another area and did the unthinkable with his service revolver. He actually lived for about two hours. He was overheard crying out to God for help. The medical doctor examined him and could not find anything wrong except that he had shot himself in his temple area. This was the horrible blow that changed life for the whole family forever. It was a huge bomb that exploded in our minds.

My father and brother brought him home in a closed casket. The whole town was at our house. Someone, a woman, held me close to her. I was too pained and sorrowful to even notice who she was. We held the viewing in our upstairs reception room. We used it only for special occasions or special company. This was the norm for the time; living in a small town with no funeral homes. The next day, we had a church funeral. Afterward we walked to the cemetery.

I don't remember if we had a hearse or if pall bearers carried the casket. I just remember Elio's resting place was a second level crypt. I didn't know how much he was loved. The whole town seemed to be sad. For the longest time, people were very kind and respectful toward my family.

In his last letter to us he seemed convinced that he had Tuberculosis of the trachea. Going through some of his personal effects, Al theorized that maybe an unscrupulous doctor off base planted the idea in his head, just to make money from him. Al looked into the matter hoping he could find the creep. He planned to make him pay dearly. Elio had just turned twenty-five in March. His promising life was cut short by a lie. I was just about to turn sixteen in October. I could hardly make sense of it all. I never found out whether there was an autopsy or not. I never bothered to ask.

We tried to pick up our lives, but it was impossible to do so for the longest amount of time. Even facing death he thought of me. He wanted me to have his wrist watch. He specified that in his last letter to us. How can I forget about something like that? Even after sixty-one years since it occurred, I cannot. Anyone who has lost a brother can relate to it. He will always be twenty-five years old to me -- handsome and always my protector and hero. He even wrote my parents and told them to let me continue my studies, even if he had to pay for them.

For months afterward, when I was alone, pasturing our animals in the fields, I would hope that this tragic event was all a dream. I hoped that at any time, he might appear, walking toward me. I guess I was in denial. In time, much later, I had to face it. I can testify of this fact to anyone. If you love your family, if you do not want them harmed, don't even let suicide enter your thoughts.

I guess when you are in a particular frame of mind, you are blinded and cannot even imagine what you are about to inflict on the ones you love the most. I once read or heard a phrase "murder by suicide." This is probably what they must have been talking about. I don't really know how it was used or even by whom, but suicide is toxic to anyone left behind. I wonder if my brother knowingly would have inflicted so much hurt on all of us had he known in advance what he was going to do. It was another tragedy my family had to endure.

While I don't want to dwell on the matter of Elio any longer, I must say one more thing about it. As I was visiting the cemetery one day, I was all alone. Even in the distance, there was no one in sight. As I stood in front of Elio's crypt, I was thinking of how much I missed him. Suddenly, I started to sense something good. It was as if a presence of peace was upon me. I could feel it deep in my soul. I did not cry. I just enjoyed the moment. There was a sense of happiness. For a while, I thought I might have imagined it, but it really happened. I never told this to anyone except my wife recently. Maybe it was a sign from above. I took it as God's way of helping me to bring closure to that chapter of my life.

That summer I tried to go on with my studies and help out on our farm. Often I would go to the reception room upstairs to be alone so I could study. My mother would follow sometimes. We had a portrait of Elio on the wall. My mother would come up and would cry and open the wounds all over again. I would get mad at her. I didn't want to see her destroy herself in that manner. Plus, she would change my mood also. On the other hand, I also felt bad for her. By now we had forgotten about America. We had tried but failed before. Now it was time to go on with our lives as best as we could. I continued my three years-in-one year study. The pressure was mounting. I needed to accomplish this. I had to succeed so that I could put an end to that chapter of my life.

As any normal young man would, I began noticing girls. However, I was too shy and only fifteen when I took an interest in girls. Dating or pursuing anyone seriously was out of the question. I always seemed to pick the ones who were interested in someone else. Besides, I was far too busy with my schoolwork and farming chores to start a relationship.

Once I was at a movie theater where they were going to show an American cowboy movie. The movie title was "Il Cavaliere Senza Paura," or "The

Fearless Rider." I think the actor was Randall Scott. A young lady about my age, maybe a year or two older than me, came into the theater. There was an extra chair available next to her. She called out to me and invited me to sit next to her on the extra chair. She said, "I don't want this other boy to come and sit here." Now this boy I'll call Fred was my age, nice looking and all. But, he was a bit aloof and highly critical. I already had some feelings of resentment against him, which gave me even more pleasure to sit in the extra chair and thus deprive him of a seat. It was this girl who I really began to notice more often after this. I made my feelings known to her. Rosa was her name. The name was fitting. She was very pretty -- blonde with green eyes and a complexion that was as rosy as her name. She responded that she was not sure that she could measure up because my family was considered in better standing than hers. We were not rich, just self-sufficient and owned some land.

Being young, naive, and ashamed to let my family know of my interest in Rosa, I was afraid that they would tease me to no end. So, I let things cool down. Besides, I thought that she was so sought after that an older guy would win her in the end. I figured she would probably want to marry much sooner than me, given her status and age. Also, since she was so good looking and received so much attention from other boys, how could I know that she would even be faithful to me? I did not make a move to become serious with her. It was just not the right time for me. Such was my life as a 15-year-old teenager.

Chapter 6: The Invisible Hand

One evening, on October 1, 1952, my father walked into the kitchen with a startling bit of information. He had just returned from a trip to Naples. To this day, I still don't know for what reason. Apparently, while in Naples, he just happened to run into an immigration agent and they had a discussion of the family's efforts to immigrate and the consulate's denial of their passports. It was through this conversation that my father discovered that because I was the son of two American-born parents and under the age of 16, I could claim citizenship through my parents. Maybe it was because I was born while they were still citizens in 1936. The only catch was that I had to be in the United States by October 3rd at midnight, just before I turned 16 years old.

This news was quite a bombshell. There were only about two days with which to get things together. That is exactly what we did. It was certainly a close call. Without my father meeting that man in Naples, I could have missed out on immigrating to America. Yet, something or someone intervened on my behalf. It was an invisible hand that kept guiding me and opening doors for me.

It was the evening of October 1st and I decided that I would go through with it. There was no time to really think, just time to act. My father asked me if I was willing to take on the task. My mother was somewhat upset at the thought of letting me go. On the other hand, I thought of fulfilling my family's dream. So, that night we got all the documents ready. The next morning, we went to Naples to the American consulate. After what seemed like forever, I was issued an American passport that expired on October 3rd at midnight. Like I said before, it was cutting things close, but it must have been meant to be. That decision to immigrate would forever change my life.

With little time to spare, I had to be on US soil by midnight of October 3, 1952. This was so surreal for me. The transformation of my life was on its way. Here I was, a small town boy who had never been to a major city in my life -- and now I was in a race to cross the Atlantic on my way to another continent in about 36 hours. Looking back, it was like an episode of the *"Twilight Zone."*

How was I supposed to do all of this in such a short amount of time? Well, as it just so happened, a distant relative of mine was staying in town. She was from Brooklyn, New York, but staying in Baia while on vacation. Had it not been for her, the whole thing would have been impossible. Yet, everything aligned so perfectly. It was another one of those doors that opened for me, unexpectedly. She made the arrangements with her family in the United States. They were to pick me up on October 3rd at Laguardia Airport at 4:30 pm, less than 8 hours before my time was up. That is exactly what they did.

On October 2nd we grabbed a taxi for Rome's airport and sped off because we were running late. It was my father, Al, the travel agent, the driver, and me. We got to the airport late. The plane, an American tourist plane, was on the runway ready for takeoff. Then in the shuffle we lost the key to my luggage, so we had to break the lock. A stewardess came in and took me to the plane. In all of the rush and confusion, I lost track of Al. I didn't know where he was. I didn't get the chance to say good-bye to him. I felt bad about that but I had no choice. I was urged to get on board and that was what I did. Just as I sat down in my seat, the plane took off. It was another close call. It actually turned out that I would never see Al again. I wish I could have said goodbye.

Wow. It was amazing how everyone scrambled to help me out. Now, here I was with all of these strangers and I could hear no Italian being spoken. We made one stop. It must have been Milano. I saw them refuel the plane. It was dark and I had no idea where we were or where we were heading. No one had spoken to me, at least not that I could understand. I just had to go along with things and hope for the best.

When we came to the next stop I was able to read "Orly Airport, Paris, France." This is where everything began to fall apart. It was about midnight on October 2nd in Paris. We were told, or at least I understood, that we would have a layover and everyone had to go to the terminal. The plane had to be cleaned. My fear was that I would not be able to determine which plane was mine on the way back. I could miss my plane and even worse, I could miss my arrival time. The fear rushed through my mind. My passport might expire and I would be stranded. I feared the whole plan would just fall apart. I couldn't let that happen. My father spent most of his savings for this opportunity. The whole family worked feverishly just so I could immigrate to the USA and start a better life. They knew that war-torn Italy offered me little. I just had to make it on time; otherwise I could not help my parents to fulfill their dream.

By the time I walked inside the terminal and turned around to see which plane was mine, I realized that I couldn't be sure which one it was any longer. I was now very confused. I didn't know anyone who could speak Italian. Was all lost? The stakes were too high for me. I could not fail my mission. I was so emotional. Just then, someone I didn't even know came up to me and said in a somewhat recognizable Italian voice that I should not be afraid; that they would make sure that I didn't get lost. It was another example of an invisible hand holding onto me. I could breathe again. I knew I was going to find that plane and I did.

The next morning we made a stop at another airport. It was the morning of October 3rd. By 4:30 that afternoon, I would make it to New York, God willing. We all went into the terminal. It was either England or Scotland, but I was never sure of which one. Things were happening in such a frenzied way. It all was happening as if on fast-forward mode. I walked into the dining area for breakfast. I had some crackers and tomato juice. Then, suddenly, I realized that this might not be paid for and I did not have the money to cover the cost. As another couple sat down, I got up and left. They wanted me to stay, but I was too embarrassed and got out of there. I didn't want any trouble. I could not let anything hold me back. It was hard not speaking the language of the others, but I was determined to go without eating if necessary in order to not miss my flight.

Back then, the planes were propeller planes, so we had to make at least two more stops before arriving at LaGuardia. It was tense for me the whole time. I was wondering if I was going to make it to New York on time.

When we landed I was asked many questions, but all I could do was present my documents. I knew that I was on time and that was certainly a comfort to me. At LaGuardia airport, the Massucci family, the relatives who were waiting for me, picked me up as scheduled. There were at least three from their family there. It was just so amazing that Mrs. Massucci happened to be in my hometown right when I needed someone. Again, the invisible hand that kept guiding me on my journey was still on my side, making the miracle possible.

I really have to say that Mrs. Massucci was a huge part of that miracle. Without her there was zero chance of my arriving in New York on time -- before midnight of October 3, 1952. If that had happened, I would no longer be eligible to become an American citizen; at least that is what my family was told.

I have often wondered about the shock to the Massucci family when they heard of my journey. Think about it, suddenly, they receive a telegram to pick up a stranger at the airport. They could have said "no." Instead, they were very gracious and kind to me. After supper that evening, Peter, the middle son, took me for a ride to see New York for the first time at night. I could not believe all the neon lights and tall buildings. I remember passing by the United Nations building.

The Massucci's other sons were Ralph, who was the eldest, along with Paul, Jr., the youngest. He wanted to be a fireman from what I remember. Their address is forever etched in my memory -- 524 Metropolitan Avenue, Brooklyn, New York.

The two older brothers were in the dry cleaning business. They ran a plant that was the central location and a pick-up location as well. It was a convenient operation for me. I was able to help them at the dry cleaner and pitch in with the workload. Doing so made me feel that at least I was doing something to earn my keep. I did feel somewhat sorry for them as they were tight on space. They opened a cot nightly for me and I would make that my bed. After a short while, they showed me a room to rent from a friend of theirs. I felt better about having my own place. It made me feel more independent and I did not feel like a burden on the Massucci family. What I did not know until later was that my father and brother were making efforts to track down one of my father's cousins in Eastern Ohio. They were trying to set me up in a more permanent location.

The Massucci's thought of sending me to night school. I was touched and deeply respected them for the offer. The school was specifically set up for immigrants. There I met people from around the globe. What I remember best were the beautiful Spanish girls. However, there was so much confusion in the class. It was run more like a circus than a class. Hardly anyone could understand when the others were speaking. People would get up and go for smoke breaks and go to the restrooms at will. There was no order at all. I was able to understand the Spanish girls and guys somewhat. I understood them because Spanish is similar to Italian. The whole time I was there I learned almost nothing. It was a total waste of time.

I would often go along for deliveries and pick-ups with the one son Peter throughout New York. To one from the farm, New York was an exciting and vibrant city. I liked it right off the bat. When I saw people all dressed up, going down to the subways and coming up out of them, it seemed like I was part of the hustle and bustle. I soaked it all in. This was a far cry from my peaceful valley back home. After a while, I began to desire greenery, but I was still hooked on "the city that doesn't sleep." In fact, I was almost sad to leave it when it was time to move to Ohio.

There were times in my life that I certainly regretted leaving Brooklyn. My days working in that Brooklyn dry cleaners were happy days. I was treated very well by my host family. I remember listening to the radio a lot. It was on at all times. Some songs I did not understand, but I became accustomed to them. Later I found out the names of the artists. I was just beginning to explore the neighborhood where I was staying. I discovered just before I left for Ohio that there was a section of all Italians. I thought to myself, "How nice is this?" I felt so welcome there. Sometimes I wonder if I would have been happier there. I guess I will never know for sure.

Chapter 7: The Journey Continues

One day in mid to late November, the Massucci's got a phone call from my relatives in Ohio. They expressed interest in my relocating to Ohio with them. All at once, plans were made for me to move to Ohio. Again, it was Pete who took me to Grand Central Station with a letter in hand that I was headed for Eastern Ohio. I boarded the train around midnight or so. After about eight to ten hours, I reached Youngstown, Ohio.

There in Youngstown, Ohio, my father's cousin Sal, his sister-in-law, and one young daughter picked me up in a 1938 Model Ford Coupe. On the way to their home in the suburbs, I could see steel mills for miles. There were smoke stacks and steam rising from the river. The river ran with beige to brown colored water. I was amazed at how much industry we had seen on the way to their home. Suddenly, we arrived in a residential area called Struthers, Ohio. I was pleasantly surprised by the green lawns, the well-manicured hedges, and brightly painted single homes with driveways. It looked like a storybook scene. The greenery was such a welcome sight to me after the cement and blacktop of New York. Things there looked to be unspoiled. I was in awe. I thought to myself that this must be a totally different world. I began to ask myself, could this all be for real? There had been so many strange twists and turns in such a short time. I could hardly take it all in.

I came to find out that there were six siblings on this side of the Merola family, each living in their own separate homes, but within two blocks of each other. I thought they must get along so well. It was amazing to me. Within a week or so I met all my relatives. Yet, I still missed the big city flash and pizazz of New York already.

When I look back on how everything unfolded, I can see so many ironies in the whole story of how I immigrated. My brother Al knew a young lady from another village who had immigrated to America some time before. He had her address posted on an envelope and pinned on the wall in our kitchen. I remember that for the longest time it had never moved from there. I guess he wanted to write to her but never got around to doing it. I remember the word Ohio on the address, only it was misspelled Ochio. I thought it was a weird name, because "occhio" means "eye" in the Italian language.

When I first arrived in Brooklyn, I always thought that eventually I would get work and settle there. Things turned out differently as the young lady Al knew in Ohio actually located my father's relatives there. They lived in the same area as my brother's friend, who had now married a son of my father's cousin. It was all so crazy.

Being in Ohio for the first time, I had to learn to adjust to things there. The first thing I needed to do was learn English. Thus far I had studied French for my three-in-one year commercial course. Actually, English was required but I had settled on French because of a lack of a teacher for English in my village.

In another one of those amazing coincidences that I continued to experience, I met a guy named Tony who became a big help to me. Tony was also from Italy. His place of origin was more northeast, toward Monte Cassino where the Third Infantry Division went to fight after liberating our town from the Nazis.

Tony had found work nearby the place where I was staying at a dairy farm. Assuming that I too would have to work for my keep at Sal's home, I asked Tony if there was work for me at the farm. Sal interjected and said that they wanted me to get some schooling completed since I was only sixteen years old. I had mixed feelings about that. I didn't want to sponge off of anyone. But Sal assured me that it would be alright.

Sal was the eldest of the family and he was still single. He was still living in his parents' home. Angelo, the youngest, had already married and now had three children. He and his wife were also living with Sal. What arrangements they had with each other, I didn't know.

At first, while I was there, Angelo arranged for me to see a teacher after the regular school day to learn some basic English skills. At about four in the afternoon I would go to see this teacher. Another brother of Angelo and Sal, who lived some thirty yards up the hill, called me and wanted to talk to me. Anthony thought that I should go to school where his kids went to school. It was a Catholic school with other boys and girls about my age, or close to it. I did not question the idea. It did make sense socially. I was now going to be more in tune with my own culture. I assumed that Angelo and Sal had been advised of the matter. I did not ask. Had they any objections, I would have heard about them, at least that is what I thought. I found out much later that Anthony wanted to take me in from the start, given that he had kids about my age.

While there, for a time, all the kids treated me as a novelty. Everyone wanted to meet me and ask questions about the old country. As it turned out, they put me with the eighth grade for a while, just to see how much I knew and whether I could perform well with them. Again, the nun in charge figured that all I needed was reading and some writing in English.

Sal, the bachelor, wanted to be my guardian since he had no children of his own and the government taxed him heavily without dependents. Angelo, his wife Martha, and their three girls, lived with Sal as one family. I did the chores they asked me to do and was working evenings at the local bowling alley setting up pins. These were the days before automatic machines. I earned ten cents per game setting up pins. Between games, I mingled with the other boys. We read funny books and I learned all the lingo of the day. It helped me to assimilate better.

As the summer of 1953 came I managed to get a job at the "cleaners." I learned how to press pants and drapes. All the workers there were very friendly. Another cousin of my father was a policeman, John. He found me the job just before the school year ended. I was grateful to him for that.

Like so many times before, I just happened to cross paths with someone who could give me a hand and help me. This time it was a kid named Tino. He was the son of Italian immigrants also. He helped me learn to read. It was a relief to have someone who looked out for me and was there for me when I needed it. Tino was nice, even if he was a bit mischievous. We played pranks on each other from time to time.

Every afternoon we would go into a small room and Tino would teach me to read English. The room used to be a kitchenette. It was small and had its own steam radiator for heating. It was warm and stuffy. As often boys do, Tino liked to odorize the room with his "scent." He knew that it would drive me nuts. He would laugh afterward. I kept telling him that one of these days I would embarrass him unless he stopped the air pollution. He must have thought I was kidding. Well, one day when I could not take it anymore, I ran out of that gas chamber and burst into the classroom while holding my nose. Immediately the class roared with laughter. That day I got the best of Tino.

While there were certainly fun times, there were times that were not so fun either. There were challenges and serious moments also. Starting over in a new country with a new language and having to make new friends was very challenging. It could even be very stressful. There were even embarrassing moments like the time I called the blood mobile the "blued mobile." It was parked on the school lot. I did not know how else to pronounce the name. The class had some laughs at my expense and that was okay. I just wanted to learn the English language well so I did not have to be laughed at any longer. Generally, I would have to say that the first school year was fun.

When school ended and summer began, I was away from school and friends. That was when the reality of my situation began to set in. I started to feel more alone. I also started to notice the novelty of being in a new country was beginning to wear off. Back home, in the old country, my family was very well respected. We were not rich, but we were self-sufficient. Sure, my father owned some land, but it was to farm -- land on which to survive. Yet, people respected us. Here I was unknown. I was feeling even more vulnerable to a let-down or a failure.

A funny thing happened while I was by myself in Ohio. My brother Al and I were getting closer by mail. He would write to me about finding who might have been responsible for Elio taking his life. I was hopeful that we would get some justice for that terrible tragedy. Thinking about Elio made me miss home. When I left abruptly, I had no time to reflect on what was happening. I missed my friends back home. I thought of Rosa. What happened to her? I asked myself if I should even try to write her or not. I knew she had many boys interested in her. Since I was so far away and unable to make a commitment to her, I let it slide. Again, this seems to be another one of those events in my life that had a greater purpose. If I had pursued a relationship with Rosa, my life would have turned out differently.

That summer I started working full time at the local dry cleaner. I made some friends there. There was a delivery man, Bill Walker, who took an interest in me. He took me swimming with him a couple of times. I made a foolish mistake of not calling my new family to let them know that I would be somewhat late. That did not go very well. They thought something bad had happened to me. I had to apologize to them.

Back at the dry cleaners, things were going well. The owner liked me a lot. Randall was very kind and friendly to me. That summer I worked with a school teacher who was working to earn some extra cash. Some of our duties were to clean the machines and work with the cleaning fluids that were used to dry clean the clothing. We had to take apart the medium that filtered the cleaning fluids so it could be reused. It was a powder that would cleanse the fluid. At least, that is how I thought it worked. Often, we found dimes that people left in their pockets. We used to save them and buy cokes to drink with our lunch.

Some of the cleaning fluid could make you light headed and give your skin a tingling feeling, especially your legs. Foolish and naive as I was, I never thought of the harm when I started getting spells of lightheadedness. I didn't know what to make of it. I felt like fainting. A buzz would run up my spine and into the back of my neck. Then I felt faint and feverish. So I decided to stay home for a time, but continued to have intermittent periods of high fever.

There were hardly any cousins around. They all had jobs, baseball games to play and other summer activities. I spent much of the time in bed alone. I thought that maybe something terrible was happening to me. I prayed really hard. I don't think that anyone knew how serious it was, not even me. That evening Angelo came upstairs to ask how I felt. When they checked my temperature, it was 106 degrees F. I needed to be hospitalized. I found out later that a fever that high could do permanent damage to a person. I was admitted to the hospital with no time to spare. Again, just in the nick of time, someone was there to guide me in the right direction. It was another example of the invisible hand at work in my life.

It turned out that I was hospitalized for some kind of virus. I remember during that moment, in the late afternoon when the sun was just about to sink below the horizon, I heard a familiar sound that brought me back to my time in Brooklyn. It was a piece of music from "La Boheme" by Puccini. It was playing on the radio and my hospital roommate was listening to it on low volume. Alone and frustrated by another setback, I was unsure if I would survive. That song brought a sudden sense of nostalgia to me concerning the days I spent in New York. I remembered having much more hope in those times. I could not help but wonder if moving to Ohio was the right thing for me. After all, I was never sick or in a hospital while in New York. I began to ask myself what things would have been like if I had not moved to Ohio.

My dad's cousin Anthony, who lived up the street, theorized that the dry cleaning fluid did this to me. Others weren't so sure. Judging by the lightheaded symptoms and the other bad feelings,

Anthony was probably correct. Angelo and Martha may have thought I was being a sissy. I think they did not believe there was a serious problem. I felt that they didn't believe me because I would get sick intermittently.

The sickness was frustrating to me. I didn't even feel hungry. I now was missing home terribly, but would not dare let my family know. I didn't want to worry them after all they sacrificed to get me to America. At the hospital, the attacks, the buzzing up my spine, the faint and feverish symptoms continued. With a temperature of 106 degrees, they ran tests of all kinds. Nothing was readily found. I dropped from 135 pounds down to 115. I was losing patches of hair. I started to think maybe I wouldn't make it. Maybe I had what Elio suspected he had -- TB. But would it not show up on my blood tests? These kinds of thoughts were racing through my mind.

As it turned out, I got a letter from Al. He was mad at me because I did not write him for a long while. I didn't write him because I didn't want to send the bad news to my family. Eventually, I did write home but I played down the sickness. I felt that I had to. After three weeks of being in the hospital, I was told that I had a virus infection at the base of my brain -- right around the pituitary gland. They gave me a new antibiotic. Things got much better after that. I was able to go home from the hospital in no time. That was about September 22. Everyone was already in school when I arrived home. The neighborhood seemed deserted. The adults were working and the younger people were in school. It was very lonely.

I had become weak from the sickness. At almost 17 years of age, I weighed about 115 pounds. My waist size was 27 inches. I tried to tough it out, but it was hard for me to grasp all that had happened. From the war to my brother's death, to the frenzied way that I came to the USA with hours to spare, I started to feel a change in me. Something was different. I hated it with passion. Why could I not escape this dark cloud that seemed to hover over me? This was the worst time of my life. I think I was becoming depressed. I began to wonder if I would ever overcome it.

The hospital bill came to over $600, a lot of money for that time. For someone making 60 cents per hour part-time, it seemed like $60,000. I didn't want to ask my father for help. I thought he was cleaned out from flying me over here. Besides, the exchange rate made their money virtually worthless after the ravages of WW II.

The doctor would not let me start my freshman year of high school until I gained back some weight. He was afraid I might catch another sickness because I was so weak. So I waited until November. This was November of 1953.

While waiting to start school, a distant relative, also from Italy -- Marco was his name -- just happened to visit Anthony's house up the street. Anthony was my dad's cousin and Anthony's wife was a cousin to Marco. He suggested that I go to his house for a weekend while I waited to start school. There were other recent immigrants there too. It was then that I experienced another one of those strange events that defined the direction of my life. It was the invisible hand that kept directing me.

On a walk one morning with that distant relative Marco, he mentioned that Rachele Conte and her family lived nearby in Pennsylvania. This was the same Rachele from Italy who learned of my birth from Zia Concetta. Paulo, her son, was one of my friends in Italy when we were a bit younger. Certainly I wanted to see Paul and his family. I needed to reconnect with someone who knew me and my family. I wanted to be encouraged and do something to lift my spirit. I figured this might be a good time to take my mind off of things and visit them.

I knew that Rachele's family had moved to America almost three years earlier, but where they lived I didn't know. They could have moved to California or Alaska for all I knew. Yet, here I was just across the border in Eastern Ohio and they were about twenty miles away in Western Pennsylvania. Rachele's family consisted of her husband and two boys, Joe and Paul, whom I knew very well, and a daughter, Anna. The daughter was about two years younger than me. I remember her in school in Italy, but we never had an occasion to speak with one another.

We visited them on a Saturday and we talked for a while. They invited me to Sunday dinner and I went back the next day. It was a nice experience and I was glad that I had visited them. I returned to Ohio that weekend but never thought I would see the Conte's again. Things turned out differently as my life unfolded over the years.

Eventually, I started my freshman year at the local high school, about two months behind everyone my age. Here the kids were totally different than eighth grade parochial school. I thought they were a bit indifferent and cold, while I was shy and reserved at that point. My personality seemed to have changed that summer of 1953 due to the sickness. I used to be more daring and gutsy before the sickness.

During that school year of 1953-1954, I passed all my subjects except English. The English teacher seemed to have it in for me. I don't know what the problem was with that teacher. I had to take the course again the following year. I passed it with a different teacher. About the middle of the school year, I could sense that things were getting worse with me and my new family. Sal and Angelo's family reached a point of no return. It was established that Martha would no longer cook for Sal or me. Sal and Martha had their differences. I began to feel uneasy there. I carried on with school and my chores as usual and worked to pay off my hospital bill. It was a strange feeling, living as if nothing was wrong. We all talked normally, but the air was now tainted. There was a bad vibe around the place.

There were other incidents that gave me some clues about things in my host family's home. Something was certainly not harmonious between Martha and my guardian Sal. Sal worked third shift. As such, I did not see him that often so I never did find out what it was. I suspected that it had to do with Sal pitching in for expenses. They never told me for sure.

While this was happening, I got some bad news about my brother Al. He was killed in an accident while doing a construction project. He was recently engaged to be married when the accident occurred. This was another family tragedy. That old gypsy's words would come to haunt me once again. Was it true that she put some kind of a spell or curse on my family? The gypsy's words, "One son will make a voyage across the sea and will not find peace, and the other will die young," rang in my ears. I never believed that anyone can foretell any event, but the gypsy's words seemed to have come true just the way she predicted. I had travelled across the Atlantic to come to America. Al, at the age of thirty, had died in the accident. Elio had died at age 25. Maybe there was some supernatural force at work that the gypsy had a connection with, like a dark spirit. She was into the occult after all. I just didn't know what to think.

My world would once again be turned upside down. I was now in limbo. My situation was no longer peaceful. Without Alfonso coming to America, I was again isolated. I later found out the details concerning what happened to Al. It was March 28, 1954. Al was working alone near a sand bank. He was getting sand to build a building that would house a bulldozer. Part of the bank gave way and he was trapped. Help came too late, I was told. He was still warm, but the life was gone from him. It was another blow to the family, especially my mother. She lost two sons in two years -- Elio at age 25 and Al at age 30.

This was painful for the whole family. I had no more hope that our family would be reunited. My parents would not leave Italy to come to America now, even though that was their dream. I had a dilemma on my hands. Do I stay in the USA or go back to Italy to be with my family? I had left my course of study in Italy. Now if I left high school in Ohio to go back to Italy, I would be nowhere again. By October of 1954 I would be eighteen; I had to make a tough decision. By law, I would have to register for the draft in the USA. What was my next step?

As I entered the school year of 1955-1956, I had to have my tonsils removed. I waited for Christmas vacation to have it done. Having no insurance, I decided to have it performed in the doctor's office. So, half way through my junior year, I mounted some courage and seventy-five dollars and headed for the Youngstown Savings and Loan building on Market Street. I did not know how primitive this was going to be. I was given local injections into my tonsils area. A kidney shaped, stainless steel tray was put in my hands to hold. The cutting started and blood dripped down to my gut and I gagged. It was so gross. I thought that this would last forever. Finally, when it was all over, they sent me to the recovery room. It was just a cot in the back room. I laid there for a couple of hours and then hopped a bus home.

For about ten days I was in misery. All I could have to eat was ice cream. During this period, however, I had a lot of time to think about my future.

Sal worked the midnight shift. I didn't see much of him. Angelo also was at work during the day. The house seemed like a prison. I didn't have anyone to talk to. Martha kept to herself much of the time. She watched TV or read novels. This time was mine to contemplate my next course of action.

I was going to be twenty in October. My senior year would begin right before I was turning twenty and I would graduate in the class of '57, a few months before my twenty-first birthday. Then I might be drafted and serve another two years or so in the military. By age twenty-three, I would then be free to begin my life anew. This seemed like a huge waste of time for me. I didn't discuss my dilemma with anyone. I figured I had to do this on my own. Finally, I decided to join the US Navy. I had heard that you could finish high school while serving. This made sense for many other reasons also. I wanted to feel that I was doing something for the country that took me in. That was my way of feeling worthy of citizenship. Also, the Navy was adventurous and I had a chance to get free passage to see my family in Italy. I would also fulfill my military obligation without having to be drafted. Plus, I might learn a trade and have a chance for a better life, to name a few. It was final. That was the best course of action I decided to take.

Prior to enlisting in the Navy, I had to get a physical check-up at the doctor's office. Doctor Hall was his name, I remember. I stopped downstairs for cigarettes at the five and ten store. There I ran into a girl that I knew from high school. She worked at that store near the doctor. I had at one time liked her but for some reason I had changed my mind. Her name was Cora and she had heard that I liked her.

The next morning, she came into my homeroom with a girlfriend of hers and they brought me a picture of her. Something in me changed. When I stopped back at the five and ten store to see her again, she offered to write to me when I was in the Navy. I accepted, but I wasn't sure anything would come out of it. I thought it was strange that she now took an interest in me just as I was preparing to leave for the Navy. I knew that I was going to need to make friends, so I agreed to write to her.

As I made preparations to join the Navy, I was at peace that my bills were finally paid. During the summer of 1955 I was able to work at the local steel mill. There I started to make some real money. Luckily, I had a boss who liked me. His name was

Mr. Novak. I worked with college students who were on break for the summer. Some would continue working through the winter on weekends. I convinced my boss to let me work also on weekends. Mr. Novak was pleased with my work ethic. When there was a job to do, usually by a group of us students, I was the first to dig in. It was part of my nature. I had worked hard from the time I was a boy. I also felt when I was busy the time would fly, as opposed to working less and getting bored. Besides, I felt a sense of responsibility to my family. I told myself it was incumbent upon any individual to produce a fair day's work for a fair day's pay.

I was grateful to my father's cousin for allowing me to go to school. However, I did not sit idle either. My first summer of 1953, before I ended up in the hospital with the virus infection, I had amassed a little savings from the cleaners and working nights at the bowling alley. Another summer I painted the house, cut grass, and did other chores. It was about the time that I went to the hospital at 17 years old that Angelo and Sal said they needed money for heating oil. I gave them $117. It was all I had.

After I turned 18, I would go to work at the dry cleaner from 7 am until 3 pm every Saturday. We did mostly maintenance work on Saturdays. I packed myself a double lunch. At 3 o'clock I would walk across the street and work at the mill until 11 pm. I repeated this schedule every weekend. On Sundays after church I would again work 3 pm to 11 pm. Monday it was back to school as usual. It was a grind but it was the only way to keep moving forward.

It was late 1955. It had been just over three years that I had been with my cousins. Now I felt that it was time to break loose. Maybe they were as tired of me as much as I wanted a change. Quitting high school was unpleasant. I really hated to do it. I was never the type to quit anything. But breaking away would be good for me. I was just going through the motions and getting nowhere fast.

Breaking free helped me to gain some confidence and self-respect that I had lost during my extended illness that first summer in America. I didn't even know what had happened to me. I felt so different after those three weeks in the hospital. I must have developed an inferiority complex. Deep down, I knew who I was. My family had a good name. We were respected in the community. But here, in Ohio, people didn't even know who I was. I even experienced my share of bias and dirty looks, even from other Italians at times. That was painful to admit. I loved America. To be treated so poorly for having immigrated, after all that I had endured, was so shocking to me.

Sometimes in my dreams, I could see myself in Italy, only to became so upset that I was no longer in America, that it would wake me.

In spite of the dirty looks and hurtful comments, I do need to give credit to my teachers, especially those who had traveled to Italy and to other European countries. They appreciated history and the arts and sciences. They didn't make me feel like I was a second class kid who happened to be an immigrant. Actually, most Americans were very kind and in awe of my accomplishments. While I did encounter some who hurt me, I swore to myself that I would show those bullies someday that I was as good as they were. This gave me greater impetus to study harder. I wanted to prove them all wrong.

A person once had the gall to ask me if I had received the "care packages" that they had sent to me during the war. True, some people devastated by the war needed those packages. So would anyone from any country that was so devastated. My family was lucky that we didn't need them. When we had to run from the Germans and hide, we did have some food shortages, but they were temporary. I was stunned when asked about the care packages. I didn't know what to say. It was very cold and insensitive. They made me feel like I was less important than they.

Another case arose as I was deciding what to make in wood shop in high school. The teacher, knowing that I was from Italy, suggested an ash tray. Another student commented, "Why an ash tray? They don't have cigarettes there." That teacher became so furious he grabbed that student and put him up against the wall. He asked the student, "What do you know about those people -- who have been through hell by war and destruction?" The student turned red faced and never spoke a word about it anymore. I was surprised because the teacher was of German ancestry. Maybe he felt a sense of empathy for me. I realize that some things are said off the cuff and never meant to hurt, but at times they do. I tried to remind myself that America is not the only place where these things occur.

I have come to find that ignorance is a worldwide problem. It is a very common human phenomenon that continues to disrupt the lives of people everywhere. I am sad to say it, but it seems that as long as there are people in this world, there will continue to be ignorance. Human beings are fallible after all.

Chapter 8: Exploring the World

After I joined the Navy with two other enlistees, we traveled to Pittsburgh for our physicals. There we met with other enlisted men and went on to Chicago by train. Ultimately, we made our way to the Great Lakes. There we were processed and had our hair cut. We looked like skin heads when it was all done. After the haircuts, we lined up to receive our uniforms and linens. I remember the mothball smell on every item. It was a peculiar scent.

Later, in the late evening, when it was around 9 or 10 pm, we were taken to a large barracks building to sleep. A seaman whose rank was E-3 was assigned over us as officer of the day. He warned that when he came back to check on us he didn't want to hear any talking or chatter. On his next round, when he entered, there was some chatter on one end of the building. He barked out, "Let's cut the crap off!" Just then, someone answered, "What's that, your head?" There was an immediate roar of laughter. He got so mad that he turned the lights on and gave us a strong warning that if it happened again we would all be sorry. But he never did come back. It was just a funny moment between all of the new recruits.

It was not long after that when companies were formed. We finally had our own barracks. The rules and restrictions were rough. We did a lot of marching in deep winter weather and cold temperatures. Our barracks were just beyond a meat packing house and a railroad. For some reason I never saw humans at the packing house. I did see what appeared to be sides of beef on meat hooks and some sort of conveyer line. That was the best I could make of things from where I was located. We were located beside other barracks and other recruits. It was such a lonely environment. It felt as if I was in jail. We were confined to barracks and confined again within the camp. A feeling of loneliness came over me. What in the world had I done? Here I was four thousand miles from my real home and a thousand from my adopted home in a strange land and strange environment. I was now with strange people whom I had not seen before. I hoped that I did not make a mistake.

The next day, as we began to mingle with one another, I finally felt like part of the group. We attended classes and marched everywhere until we had enough companies marching together in a huge hall that could hold a battalion. For some reason I found marching fun. Some recruits got blisters on their feet and others had shin splints, along with various foot problems. I never did have any problems with the marching. I think that I was used to walking from my days on that farm back in Italy. I used to cover a lot of ground with my sheep. In fact, I did walk a lot before coming to the USA and even after I landed in the USA. I still remember walking to school many times. On weekends I walked about a mile to go open the dry cleaner at 7 am. The frost used to form in my nose in the winter. I guess I was toughened by all of my past experiences.

I was often lonely in the Navy, but mail from Cora and some cousins helped keep my morale up. Boot camp turned out to be a two-edged sword. On one hand, they were breaking you down, while on the other hand they were building you up. It seemed like forever, but we did reach graduation time, sometime around mid-March. The duty stations were assigned. Mine was the sixth fleet, which included the Atlantic and the Mediterranean. That was good news for me as I had a chance to visit Italy. It seemed like that invisible hand was working on my behalf once again.

The ship I was assigned to was scheduled for a cruise to the Mediterranean. The whole company was rooting for me to make it back to Italy. That made me happy. I was proud to be in the Navy uniform. I wore it everywhere. I was now a member of the US Armed Forces -- the very US Armed

Forces that liberated my town from the Nazis and saved our lives back in 1943. I held my head up high while wearing that Navy uniform.

Wearing my Navy uniform, I went home to Eastern Ohio on leave for about a month. I was staying at my father's cousin Anthony's house now. I did go visit Sal and Angelo and family, two houses down, but I did not want to stay there any longer. We were cordial with each other, but nothing else was discussed. It was my new residential family that gave me the send-off party when I joined the Navy. I was grateful for that. They had boys close to my age as well as two girls. I was at the same home three years earlier when I was home from the hospital. There I had met my distant relative, Marco, the one who took me to Western Pennsylvania in 1953. He was a cousin to Anthony's wife and distantly related to me. Through him, I was reconnected to Rachel Conte's family and that crazy pal of mine, Paul Conte.

Catching up with my cousins while home on leave, I found out that Anthony's wife, Jen, had a sister and other family in Western Pennsylvania. It turned out that her sister was hospitalized. They were going to go visit her in Pennsylvania. They asked me if I wanted to go along. With nothing else to do, I said "yes." Here again, another one of those "meant to be moments" occurred. When we got to the hospital in New Castle, PA, I noticed across the hall from Jen's sister was another woman. Standing with this woman was her future son-in-law, who was none other than Paul Conte, my friend and Rachel's son whom I had run into three years earlier. We were both surprised to see one another. I would see Paul and his family again a few years later.

My leave came to an end and I departed for Norfolk, Virginia. On the plane before we landed, I could see that everything was in bloom and the grass and trees were alive with a beautiful green. It felt like I was in another world. Coming from Ohio where it was still winter, only to be in Virginia where it was very pretty, felt like a paradise. I fell in love with the state. People were nice at the base too. I felt free again.

There at the Navy base we trained for ship board duty. We had liberty almost every night and made some friends. We were sent to a lot of firefighting schools. We would fight fire in steel buildings just as aboard a ship. The buildings were filled with water and then fuel oil was lit on top of the water. Some gunnery school was also included. About the end of May we were loaded on buses and made our way to the Philadelphia shipyard. There we boarded the guided missile cruiser for the first time. It was great getting to know all about the ship.

My group that I had volunteered for was responsible for the ship's appearance. We made it sparkle.

Philadelphia was the great "Liberty City." People there were very nice as well. There were all sorts of programs for us to enjoy and we took advantage of it. I became so accustomed to the city that even after we left it I would go there for weekends from Norfolk, VA at times. There were so many things to do. No other port I visited was as nice as Philadelphia. When we left there for good with our ship, I really felt a sense of loss. I hoped to have stayed there a little longer. However, duty called and we did what was asked of us.

A cruiser is a ship somewhat smaller than a battle ship. Its primary function is to provide air defense for aircraft carriers. In that era when I served, guided missiles were state of the art. Our ship was equipped with terrier missiles. It had two launchers, in addition to eight inch gun turrets, five inch guns, as well as three inch/50"anti-aircraft batteries in all. The ship had quite a history. It was hit in the Pacific, around the Solomon Islands during WWII as the U.S.S. Pittsburgh. This was funny to me years later as I ended up living near Pittsburgh, PA. The ship was brought back to port and later retrofitted with guided missiles. There was much publicity about it. Miss Philadelphia came onboard for a photo shoot one day and all the newspapers carried the story. We felt really proud to serve on such a ship. The story of President Eisenhower being on our ship was carried in the newspapers back in the USA. Some people from Ohio even wrote me about it.

Due to something that happened during the war in the Pacific, an Australian ship sank mysteriously. The story was kind of sketchy, but some think that the Australian ship was sunk by mistake by our Navy. As a gesture of respect or sympathy, the former U.S.S. Pittsburgh would now be known as the U.S.S. Canberra, the Australian capital. That was what I was told, at least. It was during that summer of 1956 that we had a new guided missile cruiser commissioned. Between what they called "shakedown cruises," to test for seaworthiness, we enjoyed the liberty at Philadelphia. There were dances at the YMCA right by City Hall. On the ninth floor terrace, we had loads of fun. In that area, there were so many parks and historical sights to visit like the Franklin Institute, the Liberty Bell, and numerous art museums. We got to see them all for free. We could sleep at the Salvation Army or the YMCA on weekends for a small fee that included a continental breakfast.

While still in port, the ship was organized into departments and divisions. We all had duties accordingly. Being new and not knowing what to expect one morning, our division officer was asking for volunteers for an exclusive group. I was not quite sure what it was, but it sounded like a chance to do something exciting and new. I put my hand up and became one of the group's members. We made sure that the ship always looked good. Whatever it needed, we did it. You might say, we kept it in "ship shape." Our group was small but we worked closely together. We had liberty every night and never had guard duties. We were like a family.

Our next mission was to go show off our state-of-the-art ship while in the Caribbean. We visited most of the islands there, including Cuba; this was before Fidel Castro came to power. We visited Puerto Rico, Jamaica, Haiti, and then on to Sao Paulo, Brazil. My friend Joe from Rhode Island had an aunt living in Sao Paulo, so we visited with her family for a couple of days.

One of the most memorable times on the ship was when we crossed the equator. The guys on board had a nickname for those who had never crossed it before. They called these people a "Polliwog." As far as those who had already crossed the equator they were called a "Shellback." All the Shellbacks would round up the Polliwogs and they would appear in front of the court of "King Neptune of the Deep." Polliwogs were charged with the crime of "Being a Polliwog," whereupon the court would decide a just punishment. This was much like joining a fraternity. This lasted all day. You might receive a number of lashes, or a pretend dentist would look at your teeth and spray a bitter medicine in your mouth. Some would have to endure being enclosed in a casket or hosed with salt water. There were many other weird things like that. However, the next day we had to clean the whole ship. That was no fun at all. Eventually, we received a Declaration of Acceptance into the Order of Shellbacks.

Another memorable sight was passing near the spillway of the Amazon River. You could see the ocean suddenly split into two distinctive colors. This was by no means a small body of water. It is huge, going on for many miles. It was breathtaking to see.

By the time we returned to our home port of Norfolk, Virginia, we were given some leave for the Christmas and New Year's season. I did get to see Cora and my American family from Ohio. It was nice catching up with them. I think Cora was waiting for some serious commitment from me. I could not give her a definite answer. I was just not sure. I let things between us linger a bit as I continued to serve in the Navy. I wasn't sure when we would return to the states.

By the spring of 1957, we did return to the USA and I remember as with any ship, it needed to be put in a dry dock and inspected for repairs. When we did dry dock again, railroad cars began pulling along our ship on the pier. Work details were forming and we began to carry supplies aboard. There was a hush all over the ship. No one knew where we were going. All sorts of speculations were mounting. Some speculations were kind of funny. I remember one in particular. It said, "We are bringing a load of Vaseline to the Virgin Islands." There is always a wise guy that comes up with something like that. Eventually, we did hear something that made sense. We were to take President Eisenhower to Bermuda. There he would confer with Prime Minister McMillan of Britain. Because our President had an upper respiratory infection, we would take him into the Gulf of Mexico for some R&R for a few days. That is just what we did.

When we arrived there I remember being surprised at the beauty of the water. It was so clear there. You could see fifty feet deep or more. I had never seen water so blue and clear. We even prepared to have a swim party. The ship was at anchor. Just as I put on a swim trunk, a shark appeared. That was the end of the swim party. I never did get to swim in the Gulf of Mexico.

The President got to enjoy watching some exercises involving drones that were shot down by our missiles. We also trained with our guns and shot at a floating target towed at a distance. On one of those days he ate chow with the crew of the ship. Our captain brought him along and on the way back to his quarters our captain introduced my group of about four to him. We smiled and nodded our heads. He did the same. We were in awe. For me, this was very special. Eisenhower was the general who commanded the US Army in all of Europe during WW II. It was that same US Army that liberated our town from the Nazis. Meeting him made me feel so proud to be an American citizen serving in the United States Navy.

Sometime after the Presidential cruise of March 1957, I was with the group that was responsible for the ship's exterior appearance. While on that assignment I read something on the "plan of the day," which was our daily bulletin. There were often announcements for different schools and learning programs. I would have liked school for dental tech, but that would mean no Mediterranean cruise. Another school of learning that was offered was electronic technician. I wanted that one badly, but in order to qualify, you must have had high scores on certain tests. I happened to be just above average in these tests. The Head of Operations,

Lieutenant Pearlman, suggested that instead of electronic tech, maybe I should take "O.I.", or Operations Intelligence. This just happened to be a position as a Radarman and Radioman. The lieutenant then welcomed me aboard and told me that he hoped that I would do as well as my countryman Marconi, referring to Guglielmo Marconi, who made the first ship to shore transmission with his wireless radio. I was both surprised and touched by his comment.

After meeting President Eisenhower, we were able to make our way ashore in Bermuda. We had a few days of liberty. What is memorable to me is that it was clean and beautiful. We all rented motor bikes and had to be careful because they drive on the left side of the road. A couple of friends and I visited a lighthouse. It was kind of neat. I thought I would like to return there someday, but never have.

The other place I would like to see again is an awesome view that stretched from the Port of Santos up the mountains and toward Sao Paulo. You could see blue sea below and a panorama of Rio in the distance. The iconic Jesus with open arms was also visible.

Later that summer of 1957, we received orders to participate in an exercise with other NATO forces in the Arctic. That was the roughest sea that I saw anywhere at any time. We had waves as high as thirty feet or more. The cold was brutal. Those exercises lasted about sixty days. It was a major exercise with many other nations. We actually lost three pilots. The water was so cold that you could only live three minutes if you fell into it. The ride in the ship was brutal. The ship would rise above the water and then slam back down. As I watched it go down and heard it creak, I was afraid it would not come up again. 20,000 tons of steel now looked like a matchbox against that Artic water. Somehow, we made it through.

When we were returning from the Arctic we headed south and passed through the English Channel. Everyone went on deck to see the "White Cliffs of Dover," a landmark that pilots used when returning from their bombing missions during the war. Seeing them meant that they had made it home safely. As we were passing through the English Channel, four other sailors and I were given a birthday party. Each month they would gather a group whose birthday was close to that date and they had cake and ice cream. My age just happened to be twenty-one, the legal drinking age. That's one you remember forever, not that I was hung up on booze or anything. It was just a memorable experience. That was the beginning of our Mediterranean cruise.

We also participated in the 350th anniversary of the founding of Jamestown, VA. With other ships from NATO countries, we sailed up the James River in review. It was during this period that I made the move to O.I. Division. Being the newest member of that division, I was elected to serve in the mass cooking group for a period of 90 days. Each division would send one member so that the mess hall was always staffed. Not too many liked that 90 days of kitchen work. I for one hated it. I could not wait for it to end.

Then there was a bulletin by the Commander of the Atlantic fleet. He wanted every ship to find the sailors who could play soccer and let them join a team. This was a mandatory order. Being that I knew a bit about soccer and wanted to get out of mess hall duties, I joined such a group. Just then, a lieutenant from my division came to see me. He informed me that I was scheduled to go to radar school. This was to be great for me, I thought. I did want to go to radar school, after all. However, the word mandatory meant that my soccer obligations could not be overruled, even for radar school. This was a letdown for me but it actually worked out in a way I could not have imagined. It was another turn of events that worked out for my good.

The idea of forming soccer teams was so that we could play NATO Navy teams and make them feel at home. In most NATO member countries it was the sport they played. I got out of mess hall cooking duties, but it cost me radar school. But here is the twist. Had I gone ashore for radar school, I might have missed the Mediterranean cruise and therefore I would have missed all the ports that we visited including the time I spent in Italy with my family. There was that invisible hand guiding my path once again.

It seems that I have had more twists and turns then I can count in my life. Maybe this is life for everyone but I am not sure. I sometimes wonder about how things may have turned out if I went to radar school. All the events that followed depended on that one change from radar school to playing soccer. It's crazy how so much hinges on a few decisions.

The rest of the movement through the Mediterranean was as if I had hand-picked it. First we made stops in Barcelona, Spain, then on to Turkey. I visited Ephesus and the Roman ruins, then Istanbul, Greece, Crete, and Athens. We went to see the Acropolis with my friend Nick and celebrated my becoming a petty officer there.

When we stopped in Naples, Italy, it was just in time for Christmas and the New Year. After five years, I finally got to see my family, at least what remained. Things that I remembered as big now seemed small. The piazza where Paul, my friend from Western Pennsylvania and I had played, now seemed so scaled down. Things had changed somewhat in town, but not drastically. Some friends of mine were in Switzerland, Canada, Germany, France, and other countries. Work was scarce and people moved around to find a job.

Each port we visited etched some memories in my mind. The one port of call that I can't forget about is Largs, Scotland. I recall coming north along a rugged and beautiful coastline. What deeply impressed me were the rolling hills and knolls. The vegetation was such a vivid green that it looked like a never ending carpet of lush and uniform velvet. When we came ashore I was even more impressed. I marveled at the number of red haired people in the crowd. It was easy to spot them at once, and of course, the men wearing kilts. I noted to Joe Pesare, one of my friends, that I had met Italians in every port we visited, but doubted if we would meet one here in Scotland. Just then, walking down the street, we spotted a neon sign in large letters that said, "Nardini's Restaurant." How about that? This is a mere observation and to be taken only as such, but it was true. I found Italians in Cuba, Brazil, Greece, Turkey, Spain, and many other places.

While in Scotland, two friends and I met three Scottish girls and convinced them to have something to eat in the restaurant nearby. We chatted for the longest time as we ate. When I ordered iced tea, I was surprised that the tea came in a large cup but was hot. I guess they didn't use tea as an iced drink. We chatted for so long and eventually ended up at one of the girl's house. We ended up chatting even more with the family until late. It was nice visiting that family. Norma was the name of the girl that I liked. Someone in her family talked about when he was in the British Navy during WWII. He wasn't very happy with it. I was surprised that there seemed to be some resentment toward the Brits.

Norma and I actually wrote to one another for a while, but as time passed, things cooled down and I lost touch with her.

When in Spain, we visited one of their islands called Mallorca. We had to travel by boat at one point. I had a very memorable experience there. Sitting in the boat and across from me was a young man that I almost thought was my brother Al who had died a few years earlier. To this day I still think of that encounter. While I was looking at this man, I wanted to dream that maybe what happened to my brother was all a mistake and that maybe now he was in Spain or Mallorca. That dream turned to reality when I had to admit that he was not really my brother.

Barcelona was a nice port to visit also. We wanted to see a bullfight if we could. For a time there was talk of it. However, it was out of season. My friend Dave and I did visit the bullring. Unfortunately, or fortunately for the bull, there was no fight. Because of my Italian knowledge, both regional dialect and proper Italian language, I could navigate easily with Spanish and Portugese. I could even understand some French, but not well. I did study French for three or four months. I found it to be harder than Spanish. David and I met two Spanish sailors while in Mallorca. While I spoke with them, I found out that while in Barcelona we had visited one of the sailor's local neighborhood. So we decided to spend an evening together. When we had dinner together at a restaurant, David and I were going to pick up the tab. They, in turn, insisted on paying for us instead. So we spread good will and friendship. I had made friends in every Spanish speaking port.

I did study my books and eventually passed my Radarman test. With two friends, we celebrated my promotion to Petty Officer Third Class in Athens, Greece. After Greece I was able to take leave in my hometown for Christmas of 1957 and New Year's Day 1958, in Italy. I met the mother of a girl that Al had dated for a while. She let me know that Netta was now in America, about 20 miles from Eastern Ohio, in Western Pennsylvania in New Castle, PA. She said that I should go see her. In fact, she made me promise that I would. This visit, as we will see, changed life for me once again. It was one of those paths that I was supposed to take. The invisible hand that kept guiding me was at work even in this seemingly small event.

After leaving Naples we stopped at Gibraltar. At Gibraltar, we went on a short tour with a few friends in a taxi. We visited the upper most part of the Rock. It was just rock; totally barren. There were all these baboons with bare butts. I had never seen baboons this way. The taxi guy told us that according to tradition, the English kept them there believing that as long as they remained there, the Rock would always be in English possession.

After Gibraltar we entered the Eastern Atlantic. The ocean was a bit heavy. They say that traveling from east to west is always harder due to the rotation of the earth.

My duty station was below deck sometimes. Other times I was on the bridge or C.I.C., Combat Information Center. As we were traversing the Atlantic one day, I was at my duty station below deck. On a piece of radio equipment, we heard an

American song. We were elated to be in touch with America once again. The song went something like this: "26 miles across the sea, Santa Catalina waits for me, romance, romance, Santa Catalina the Isle of Love," etc. You don't forget things like that in those moments of time. It gives you a lift. And so it is that I can still remember. My heart was yearning for America, but I felt a little bit sad for leaving my family behind again in Italy. It was after that, although how long I don't remember, that we docked in New York. Again, there were a lot of festivities. Arlene Francis, a TV personality, came aboard and we were on TV. I happened to be below deck at my detection and tracking station when she did. I didn't get to see much of the hoopla. It was Armed Forces Day celebrations, so there was much ado.

From there most went on liberty or leave. I left for leave and returned to Eastern Ohio and my American family. I asked my cousin to drive me to Western Pennsylvania to see Netta. I had promised Al's ex-girlfriends mother that I would visit her. I got the feeling that she, the mother, may have had hopes for Netta and me to date. When we arrived in New Castle, PA, at her aunt's place, Netta was not at home. I explained to the aunt who I was and why I was there. The aunt made known to me that she was out with a boyfriend. I figured what's the point in trying to reach her if she has a boyfriend? From that point on, I was off the hook.

Since Rachel's family lived nearby, I decided to visit with them. I had not seen them since 1953. It had been about five years since I first visited the family. I had seen my pal Paul once at the hospital when I was home from boot camp in March of 1956, but not the rest of the family. As I knocked on the door, I found out that they were as happy to see me as I was to see them back in 1953. What I liked most was the looks of that fifteen-year-old girl, Paul's younger sister, Anna. I thought I might luck out and see her again. As I walked up the front steps, there she was, a beautiful young lady. I liked her at once. She made me feel that she was someone I wanted to settle down with right from the start. Anna was going to be 20 years old and I was going to be 22 years old. I had thought that by now she was either married or had a steady boyfriend. It happened that she was writing thank-you notes to people who had attended her high school graduation party and was including her picture in every note. I thought it was worth taking a risk to ask for a picture. When she did not object, I made another request. I asked her if I could write to her and asked for her address. She pointed at the house numbers on the wall. That was all I wanted, for her to give me a chance.

I came to find out later that she had other boyfriends at different times. For some reason or another she did not have one at this time when I saw her on the porch. I too had some girls I dated, but never made any commitments. After that first visit, when I got her picture and address, I came back to her high school prom with another young lady. She was also graduating and was a friend of Anna. Her boyfriend was in the Coast Guard and could not come home to take her. In fact, her friend enticed me to take her to the dance with the hope that I would see Anna there. I had sent a telegram to ask permission from our Captain to extend my leave for a few days. I was surprised to receive the ok from him. However, I did not get to see Anna at the dance. I did speak to her on the phone after the dance.

After I left for Norfolk, I found out that we were going on another cruise. This one would be for Sweden and a few other ports. I think I may have written to Anna during this cruise. However, when we got to Vigo, Spain, during that cruise, I got bad news. My mother had died on June 14, 1958. At first I was stunned. Then I went off by myself and cried my eyes out. The Division Commander found out and came to see me. I can't remember his name, but something tells me his last name was Gates. He was very nice to me. God bless him wherever he is now.

It was arranged for me to fly to Morocco by mail plane. There was an Air Force base there and some Navy presence as well. From there connections were made to fly me to Naples with a stop at Malta. I was too late for the funeral, but I spent a month there with my family which now shrunk to three. I didn't want to believe it, but I intuitively knew my mother would eventually succumb to a heart attack. After she lost two sons in two years and one son was so far away, her heart just gave out. My brothers were 25 and 30 years old when they died. Any mother would be just as broken hearted. I was grateful to have seen her just about six months earlier. It was another event that was guided by that invisible hand. Had I not joined the soccer team, I never would have been able to go to Italy and see my mother before she died. She had asked me if I had a girlfriend. To put her at ease, I told her that Norma Lowry and I were writing to each other. While this was true, it was only partially true. Norma and I had already started to cool things off. I didn't want to say anything to my mother about it. She seemed ok with the fact that I was writing someone. I guess parents always want to see their children settle down.

As time slipped away from my thirty days leave, I reported to Naples at the U.S. Navy base. After a few more days there, I met other sailors waiting for passage back to their duty stations in the U.S. or ships and bases. Our superiors made us do some light chores while we waited. It was mostly cleaning our quarters and moving materials around. I noticed

a few Philippino-American sailors who would look at me with a grin on their faces. Then, they would utter some Italian words in a song. At first I didn't know what the meaning of the song was all about.
Then, after some time, I heard an Italian song by Domenico Medugno called "Volare." Apparently, they figured I was of Italian origin and wanted to see my expression to the song. That song turned out to make the number one spot on the charts for forty-one weeks straight during that summer of 1958. Everyone asked me what it meant. It really was beautiful. The lyrics were poetic and the sound of the music had a catchy magic about it.

After about a week we got a flight directly to Charleston, South Carolina. We had sailors, Marines, and civilian dependents aboard. From there I made my way back to Norfolk, where my ship was in port.

When I got aboard, I found some mail. Among my mail was a sympathy card from Anna and her family. When I found Anna's sympathy card, I was as surprised as I was thrilled that she cared. Slowly I started to write to her and even called her on the phone a few times. I can't recall how I found out that her birthday was coming up. My friend Nick and I went on liberty one evening. The bus station was in front of a Grants' Five and Ten store. While we waited for our bus to take us from Norfolk to

Portsmouth, I went inside. I looked to find a card that she might like. Nick came looking for me and asked how long it takes to get a birthday card. Finally, I came across a card that expressed my deep feeling. It had a honey bear on it. It was quite charming, so I picked that one to send. When I got an answer from Anna, I knew that I picked the right one. She said, "That's the nicest card that I ever received from anyone before." She commented that I must have searched for a long time to find such a sweet card. Things started to get more serious between us.

Through our letters, I learned that we had some common feelings for one another. I had promised myself that I would never marry an Italian girl. I thought that Italian girls were argumentative and to be blunt, quite mouthy. I am sure I came to that conclusion due to my own experiences. I always felt that way. Maybe it was all the arguments that I had with my sister growing up. My sister was good and kind, but with me she thought that she had to be the boss because she was three years older. I used to hate putting up with her mouthy attitude. I must have thought that taking flak from her made me feel like less of a worthwhile person or something. We had many fights and disagreements, but we made up just as easily, which was a positive thing.

Ironically, Anna thought that all Italian males were chauvinists. Being the only girl and the youngest of the family, I can understand how she might have felt while growing up. When her family came to America, the brothers worked hard and paid room and board. Her parents had built a new home and the loan had to be paid. That being the case, much of the work around the house fell on her even though she attended school full time. The boys seemed to think that since they worked and paid room and board that they didn't want to hear about the rest of the housework.

Eventually, Anna and I got to know each other better and all of these stereotypes disappeared.

Anna used to ask me about an incident that happened before either of us had come to the U.S. Back in Italy, I used to see her in school. I knew that she was Paul and Joe's sister but never had any occasion to talk to her. She seemed quite reserved and maybe a bit aloof. One day before classes, I was playing street soccer with the other kids. The ball had rolled near where she was waiting for her girlfriend. I was curious about her. I was trying to sum her up. Without any hesitation, I gave her a once-over look. I wanted to see what she was all about. I had forgotten all about it. She, on the other hand, had not. She proceeded to tell me that she felt like saying, "What are you looking at?" It was strange. Never in a thousand years did I think that I would fall for that girl whom I was sizing up during grade school all those years later -- and in America. She still kids me about it. I recall only vaguely where it took place. She, on the other hand, tells me just where it was. I do admit that I did that, only I cannot remember the location.

Connecting with Anna thousands of miles from home was an amazing thing for me. It all happened because I promised to visit New Castle, PA while in Italy for New Year's Day of 1958. Then, when home on leave months later, the girl that I was supposed to visit was out with her boyfriend. Having nothing to lose, I visited her family in hopes of seeing Anna and I did. It had been about 6 years since I saw her last. Had I not been in Italy for the New Year, I would probably have not made that promise. Had I not made that promise, I probably would have not been in New Castle when Anna was writing thank you cards for her graduation party. It all just fell into place.

Chapter 9: Making Life Count

By the time that I had served about thirty-five months of my forty-eight month enlistment, my health started to suffer. My mother's sudden death was the final straw for me. It was like a balloon had popped in my soul. The stress and anxiety had caused me to get ulcers and I had contracted a skin condition as well. Stress and anxiety can do destructive things to a person's health. I looked back on my life and could see how things had moved so quickly. It was like a big fast freight train ride. Now that freight train had come to an end with a collision caused by my mother's death.

I had to take a hard look at things. From the time I was a boy and lived through WW II, to the stress-filled way that I was rushed into immigrating to the USA right before my sixteenth birthday, to the deaths of my brothers and mother, it all happened like a whirlwind. Things had been so crazy for me that I didn't have time to take a breath. I really needed to take that breath and start over. The anxiety was eating away at me.

After a consultation with the medics, it was decided that I needed a more stable life as a civilian and some counseling to get back on my feet. I received an honorable discharge -- for medical reasons with time served. I had served three years in the US Navy. I was proud to have served those three years in the Navy. It was a lot of fun but it was no vacation either. We were always busy at sea. It helped the time go by so you didn't think about how lonely it could be. We served in shifts around the clock, cleaned our compartments, and painted a lot. We had drills of all kinds. We tracked other ships and aircraft, navigated our own ship, provided meals, and ran all departments. We manned battle stations and kept our decks clean. When we were on a cruise, we saw water and skies for months at a time. There were many other jobs to perform, far too many to mention.

If I had my youth and my health back, I would do it again without hesitation. I think that the military turns boys into men. It is a good experience for just about anybody. My military experience was good for me. It just happened to occur at a difficult time in my life.

After leaving the Navy, I made my way back to Eastern Ohio. After two to three weeks of civilian life, I was fortunate to get my job back at the local steel mill. I now lived with my father's cousin Anthony and his family. We agreed on a fair amount for room and board and things were working out. I was able to see a counselor and after some time my health improved. I was able to learn how to cope with the anxiety.

For most of my life, I have regretted those three years on the ship coming to an end. There were too many good friends that I left behind. They had become my family. I never discussed my personal struggles with any of them. I felt that they might not understand. Many of them I would come to miss. Even today, I often wonder what has happened to them all. I kept in touch with just two of them. The others I never saw nor heard from again.

One sailor I kept in touch with was Joe. His hometown was Providence, Rhode Island. We talked on the phone at times, exchanged Christmas cards, and even wrote letters. We never forgot the good times we had, especially our visit to Sao Paulo, Brazil. An aunt of his married a well-to-do businessman who worked in the import-export business. We spent a few days with them.

Joe and I did a lot of funny stuff too. He took 16mm movies of our fun adventures. He promised me that he would send me copies of it all, but he never got around to it.

Another memorable event with Joe was at Guantanamo Bay, Cuba. We visited that port often. We would go out to sea for maneuvers with other ships and afterward would drop anchor at Guantanamo for some R&R.

The base was like a city on its own. There were many things to do for sea-weary sailors. We could go scuba diving, play baseball, have beach parties, rent bikes, and go exploring the island. There were countless other activities as well. It was on one of those excursions that Joe and I got into some trouble.

As we rode our bikes, we met a bully from the ship. He was totally wasted. Drunk and angry, he approached me and wanted my bike. The rules of the bike rental shop were clear: if any harm came to the bike, you would pay damages. I, of course, refused to let the bully ride my bike while drunk. So we had words with him. He threatened to wrap the bike around my neck. The shore patrol happened to be a short distance away and broke up the altercation.

That evening, as Joe and I were having something to eat at the local E.M. Club, we spotted the bully with two of his cohorts. They kept staring at us from a distance. We didn't know what was on their minds but the stares were not friendly. We thought that we would have a fight on our hands. Out of nowhere we saw another sailor, Jim Slater, approach and come to sit with us. Jim was from one of the Dakotas. I can't remember if it was North or South. After the usual chatter, he let us know that he heard those three bullies had it in for us. Jim was a member of my division and we slept in the same compartment for a time. Jim also happened to like a good fight. He was big and strong. He could handle the bullies all by himself. We knew that Jim wasn't afraid to fight. Jim proceeded to tell me that if anyone wanted to harm me they would have to do it over his dead body. Since Joe and I were only two men, the three bullies were a real threat to us. Jim stayed with us all night. When we went back to the ship, all was forgotten. The bullies never again said anything. So as the saying goes, a friend in need is a friend indeed.

Once, Jim was out on liberty and came back without his dentures. He had waited months to receive them after his teeth got so bad that they had to be removed. Jim had lost the dentures in a fight. That was Jim. He remained a good friend. Wherever you are Jim, thank you for all of the good times in the Navy.

After a time, we got a new sailor aboard. His name was David Ornelas. David attended the same high school I attended in Struthers, Ohio. I actually ran into him for the first time when we were in the restroom, or "head" in Navy lingo. When we saw one another, we jumped for joy. He ultimately was attached to the same department as me as a lookout, but in a separate division. However, we worked closely together with that division. I had a lot of fun with David. What sticks out in my mind was our time in Istanbul, Turkey. David and I took a taxi to a club. As we chatted with the driver on the way, we asked the driver to help us learn some Turkish words. David was sitting in the back seat, while I was up front next to the driver. Wanting to be funny, I asked the driver, "How do you say, 'Hi, Beautiful. I love you.'" The driver told me the words that I still remember. They went something like, "Goonsel Catoon Sany Sayviorounh." I was crazy for doing what followed. When we reached a red light and stopped, another taxi pulled up next to us. I thought it was my opportunity to test what I had learned from the driver. I motioned to the taxi next to us to get his attention. Then, using hand motions, I said that our driver wanted me to tell him what I thought meant "Hello, Beautiful. He loves you." That driver gave me a look of rage. He slammed his hands on his steering wheel and took off like a rocket. Our driver looked at me and said, "No! No! No! That is very bad." I turned around but couldn't see David. He was on the floor holding his stomach from laughter. I realize now that stunt was foolish. When you are a young man in the Navy, it is easy to act foolish. You will do most anything for a laugh.

On another occasion, David and I went to another location in Istanbul. Dave got on the piano and played a short little something. These Norwegian sailors were in the crowd and apparently listening. Suddenly, Dave stopped and they would not let him leave. They wanted more. I, too, said play more. David responded with a whisper in my ear that he was faking it. I guess the piano was an automatic playing piano.

By now, we had been in Istanbul for a few days. Our money had dried up. We happened to meet a Turk that had been in America in his younger days. He spoke some English. So we struck up a conversation with him. He had a large glass of whiskey. We, on the other hand, were nursing the last glass of beer that we could buy. When the Turk went to the restroom, Dave suggested that we add some whiskey to our beer. I was reluctant. Dave thought that if we did that, we would feel more of a punch from the beer because that was all we could buy at the time. Unfortunately, the Turk caught us in the act. We were ashamed for it and apologized. But he said go ahead and help yourselves. David still lives in the area of Youngstown, Ohio. I kept in touch with him for a bit but have not seen him in quite a while.

Nick Vitelli was another good friend. We did many things together also. He once brought me to his home in what I think was Nutley, near Melville, New Jersey. I met his family and spent the weekend with them.

One memorable thing about that weekend was that we visited his godfather. His godfather was a surgeon and ex-Naval Officer. He was now married to an Italian airline stewardess and they had a daughter who was about six years old. His sister-in-law lived with them. I kind of hoped to meet her again but it never took place. Nick had bought the young girl a doll in Italy and we went to deliver it. They were very friendly and gracious people. When we left, the good doctor slipped a twenty dollar bill in my pocket. I was surprised. In 1958 that was still nice change. When Nick saw that I was surprised with a twenty dollar bill, he said, "Wait until you see what I got." His turned out to be a one hundred dollar bill.

Nick was a nice friend and we had a lot of fun together. What came as a surprise to me was that Nick and Joe didn't like one another all that much. Nick was more serious and reserved. Joe was a free spirit and perhaps a bit more of a show-off. I figured their personalities just didn't match.

I visited Nick and his wife and child with my wife

and children on our way to Italy in 1965. Nick and I went to buy some pizza. The wives and children were at home waiting. His wife confided with my wife that they had a strained relationship. It was obvious that our being there at that time was not the most beneficial thing for his marriage. My wife and I cut our trip short. We then exchanged Christmas cards for some time. Then, things faded.

Some years later while traveling east on vacation, I called Nick. I wanted to stop by and catch up with him. We chatted for a while and then he dropped a bomb. I had called hoping to see him again, but as we talked, he asked me what I wanted. I was stunned. I said that I didn't want anything. He responded that maybe I should stop to see his parents at the beach. I detected some somber feelings. Maybe he didn't want me to know that he had marital problems. I never did find out. Too bad I never did reconnect with him.

I am forever grateful to another friend, Eddie Eddings. He was a kind gentleman. He once told me that one of his best friends was an Italian. They were from Buffalo, New York. Most of the Radarmen on our ship came from radar school. On the other hand, I moved up from the hands-on training group. The ones that had schooling already had more knowledge about radar. I had to learn by trial and error and from manuals. Exams were offered for Radarman 3rd Class, or an "E-4." In order to qualify, you had to be recommended by one of the superior grades. I don't remember the details, but I was recommended by Ed Eddings without my knowledge.

When I showed up for the test, the Chief Petty Officer asked with surprise who recommended me. I didn't answer anything. I took it to mean that he did not have faith in me passing the exams. After a time, I forgot about the exams. Then one day I was on the bridge and on duty. A call came to me from Ed Eddings. He was happy and jumping for joy. When I asked what was happening, he replied, "You passed the exam for E-4. I recommended you for the exam." I had no idea that he was the one who recommended me. He was happy that I proved him right. I was happy for both of us. These kinds of things seem to be small, but it really meant a great deal to me. It's rewarding when someone has faith in you and then you succeed. That saves face for both concerned. In addition, it renews your faith in the human race. Thanks, Ed. You deserve my respect.

Another good friend was from Brooklyn. I can only remember his last name, Rago. We slept in a small compartment area of about eight or ten sailors. We became good friends. We were all like a family while I was attached to that division. Rago had a steady girlfriend back home. They wrote to each other quite often. One day he told me that he didn't know what to write to her anymore. After asking my help, I accepted his challenge. I went up on the main deck. It was late afternoon and the sun had already begun to set below the horizon. So I thought I would write about that subject. I told her that as the sun was setting, my thoughts had turned to her at home. I must have laid it on quite thick. I gave him my script and he must have sent it just as I had written it without reading it.

Later on, maybe a week or two later, I asked him how it went. He said to me, "You son of a gun, you will not write any more letters for me. The last one you wrote got me engaged." We all laughed about it. I might have told him something like, "That's what good friends are for." He never did ask me to write to her again. I can't say that I blame him.

There was another person aboard our ship whom I should have visited, but I never did -- the Captain. One day, I was assigned to demonstrate our survivor apparatus. When Captain Mauro came to look at the display, he asked me how many men could occupy each raft. When I answered "fifteen," he responded to me in Spanish, thinking that I was Spanish. I then said that I was Italian. I already knew that his family's origin was from Naples, Italy.

He then reaffirmed that his family was indeed from Naples. After chatting a few minutes, he thanked me for the good job I was doing. But before he left, he told me to come and visit him sometime. I regret that I was too much in awe of his rank and status and that I was somewhat shy. I never did stop in to see him. In retrospect, I think that could have been an interesting visit. Eventually, he was transferred and we got a new captain before I left the ship.

There are too many other people who have had an impact on my life. It's sometimes surprising who will stand out from the rest and act in good faith toward another person. Regardless of who you are, or where you are from, this type of person is worthy of being "memorable" and called a "stand-up guy," as Bill O'Reilly often says.

Sometimes in life, it's the person who gives you that one word of encouragement that inspires you to go on. They always hold a close place in your memory. Everyone needs someone like that from time to time.

Chapter 10: Beginning Again

Upon returning home from the military, I thought of continuing my education. If I could, I would have liked to have been a math teacher. Instead, I had to work as a laborer in the local steel company and hope it would lead to something better. It wasn't long before there were talks of a big steel strike on the horizon.

Tino, my mentor from eighth grade in Catholic school, was going into business with a relative of mine. He asked me if I would take over his job as a driver salesman for a local bakery. I liked the idea due to the looming strike at the mill. Unfortunately, Anna's father thought that I was lazy for giving up my job at the steel mill. Anna was already getting anxious to break loose from her father's strict control over her. My quitting my job really stirred things up with him. I had hoped for more time before we would get married, but Anna was under a lot of pressure. Her father was really making life hard for the both of us.

At first I resented the idea of getting married so soon. Here I was, almost twenty-three years old and Anna almost twenty-one. We weren't that young, yet we weren't that old either. I had to make a decision. Anna was the one I wanted to marry. She was a fine young woman and I didn't want to lose her. I considered holding out, yet the thought that I may lose her to someone else was too much to bear. She was pretty, smart, and well-mannered. She was educated in Italy and in America as well. As a family, the Conte's were rather modern and had just built a new home. They weren't like some of the other people who immigrated to the USA from Italy who had refused to assimilate. They knew they had to make a place for themselves in the USA and that is what they did. I could appreciate their culture and how they lived. That is how I had envisioned living myself someday. They had taken hold of the American dream and were living it. This was my way of thinking as well.

At first I thought it was strange that I had agreed to marry someone from not only my home country, but my hometown as well. We each had realized that although we both had ideas about not marrying within our own nationality, we had too many things in common that would prove beneficial in the long run. Ultimately, these common things would prove to be assets and not liabilities to us.

That summer of 1959 was moving along fast. We made preparations for the wedding for September 12th. We rented a small apartment near her home and got it all spruced up. It was only three rooms but we figured that was good for the time being. Anna's mother, Rachel, begged me not to take Anna to Ohio. At first, I did want to move to Eastern Ohio near my cousins, which was about twenty miles away. But Anna was rooted in Western Pennsylvania with her immediate family. Since I was not, I reasoned that I was not giving up as much as she would have to give up had she moved to Ohio.

I became aware of other things about Anna and her family. Although I knew Paul, Joe, and Anna in Italy, it never occurred to me that their father Ralph was not around. When you're young, certain things are of no interest to you. Apparently, he had already immigrated to America. Ralph and his cousin Patsy would work in the mills of Western Pennsylvania and then return to Italy for a few short years. They were both married. Ralph would marry Rachel and Patsy would marry Antoinette. After a few more years in Italy, they then returned to the USA. Patsy would take his bride with him, while Ralph left Rachel in Italy. His family wanted him to remain in Italy. They did not want him to keep traveling to America. He planned to earn some money and then go back to Italy to stay for good. As more children were born, however, Ralph made more trips to America to earn more money to support his family. Eventually, Rachel became pregnant with Anna. Ralph said that he would return to the USA just one more time and then he would go back to Italy to stay.

On his last trip, while Rachel was to give birth to Anna, hard times fell upon him. Ralph became stranded in America. Unable to bring more money home due to the Great Depression, he waited to see what he could do to go back to Italy after building some savings for himself. To his dismay, the hard times of the Great Depression lasted a long time. Then WWII came about. Because he was not yet an American citizen and Mussolini had joined with Hitler in the war, the US government ordered Ralph to an Army post in Western Pennsylvania where he worked as a cook. It wasn't ideal but it did serve a purpose. He at least had a roof over his head and plenty of food to eat. Yet, things were not working out as planned. This order by the government delayed his plans to return to Italy even more.

Meanwhile, his family in Italy struggled. Rachel now had three children to feed and no husband to support her. Their family, like mine, also had to run away and hide in caves along the river or in the mountains when the Germans came to town. Our river had some high banks. When the water flow changed course and moved away from the old bed, there was a long distance to the shore from the banks. People dug large shelters along those banks and made lodging space for themselves. My family made provisions around the foot of the mountain when the front came through our town. In the midst of the war, Rachel's house was bombed. They had to wait about two years before their home would be restored. They had to make do with Anna's grandfather's place in the meantime, even though it was not exactly roomy.

Rachel, as a single mother, did an excellent job of raising her children. It did come at the cost of her emotional health for a time. I know because as I mentioned before, I thought that Anna was more of a city slicker. By that, I mean all people who did not work the land or the farms. Manual labor was considered lower class to some people, while others understood that if you worked the land you had property and therefore you were better off than the so-called city slickers. It seemed like she was distant and not always friendly. I guess she was being protective of her family. After all, she was a single mother raising children and enduring a major world war.

Times were tough for me and my family during WW II too, but even more so for Rachel Conte and her family. Raising three kids during a major war without a husband to help was bad enough. Losing your farm to the Nazis and then having your house hit with bombs was even worse. They lost touch with Ralph for about a decade and did not even know where he was. They had no way to contact him or write him. It was as if he had fallen off the face of the Earth. Rachel and Ralph had not even been married for all that long before they lost touch. They were actually arranged to be married by their parents. Ralph's family was an upper-middle class family and Rachel's was a lower-middle class family. Pairing them together meant Rachel could move up in her socio-economic status. Unfortunately for Rachel, she was already in love with someone else other than Ralph. In the end, she did what her parents asked and married Ralph so that she and her children would have a better life. She never did reconnect with the first love of her life. Rachel's life was filled with many tragedies.

We take so much for granted these days. Most of us would never consider marrying someone for any other reason than love. Those times were different back then. People back then had to do whatever it took to survive. They found a way to make things work even when circumstances were not ideal. There was little room for mistakes. One mistake could cost you dearly. That is probably why people were so hard on their families and friends. They wanted to help them to survive.

Finally, several years after the war ceased and things began to normalize, a man who was originally from our town in Italy came to visit his family. He lived in New Castle, PA, the same town where Ralph Conte lived. Rachel knew that gentleman who was visiting our hometown. She got Anna by the hand and went to see that man. Anna by now was about nine years old. She had never seen her father. Rachel asked that man if he had seen her husband, since they knew each other in Italy as well as in Western Pennsylvania. The man said to Rachel, "Take a picture with your children and I will look for him when I go back." When that man went back to New Castle, PA, he tracked down Ralph and showed him the picture. When Ralph saw the picture of his family, he broke down in tears. He could not believe they were still alive. It had been about a decade since he last heard from them. He used to see the news reels of all the bombings in Italy and thought that they had died.

Imagine the shock that Ralph must have endured when seeing a picture of his family after all those years. I wish someone had taken a picture of his reaction.

With communications now open between the family, Ralph wasted no time. He promptly made plans to have his oldest son, Joe, immigrate to America first. Joe, now eighteen, could help his father earn some extra money to save toward the trip for the rest of the family to immigrate. Joe immigrated to the USA and began working. They saved up the money and in 1950, during the month of March, Rachel, Paul, and Anna did immigrate to America. Ralph went to meet them in New York. The "Saturnia" Passenger Lines, which he had often used himself during his trips back and forth to Italy, now brought the rest of his family to America.

While at the dock, Paul went looking for his father Ralph in the midst of a crowded group of people getting off of the ship. Somehow he found Ralph and they embraced. Ralph could not believe his eyes when he saw his children, especially Anna. She was still in Rachel's womb when he last saw his family.

Western Pennsylvania was booming with industry in 1950. Steel mills were a big employer in the area. The railroads that supported the steel mills with coal and iron ore, sandstone, and whatever else the steel mills needed were also busy. Back in those days the railroads also hired workers to maintain the rails. Work was abundant and easy to get. With the arrival of the rest of the Conte family, they could finally be a complete family. There was a twist though. Somehow, Ralph's last name was misspelled when he immigrated and his last name was no longer Conte but Conti. His children and wife accepted the change graciously and began their assimilation into the American way of life. That's just one of those things that I admired about her family.

Ralph's boys worked hard. Joe and eventually Paul paid room and board and with all three men contributing to the family income, they managed to build a modest new home. Anna, being the youngest, attended public school and was the first in the family to graduate high school. Rachel would also join the work force to help out the family. She got a job at a local green house. In the summertime, Anna would join her Mom picking produce at the farm.

Watching the newly renamed Conti family, along with my cousins, work hard and sacrifice in order to make a better life for themselves, taught me about the recipe for success. This is why so many immigrants from different countries have come to America and advanced in life. Sometimes this surprises those who have been born and raised in the USA. In my experience, some of the people born and raised in the USA come across as entitled, believing they are supposed to have a better life without much work to make it happen. Don't get me wrong, this is not the case for everyone born in America. It is just the case for some born here, but for someone who did not have the same opportunities and financial support it seems like such a shame. I wish I could have had some of those opportunities. I would have made them count if I had them.

I once was asked by a lady that I knew why an immigrant family in her neighborhood could come to America and in four years be able to build a new home, while she lived here and was forty years old and had nothing. Intrigued, I asked her how she thought they did it. She replied that the father of this immigrant family opened a barbershop. The mother worked and the children each had a newspaper route. In turn, I replied that the family was industrious and therefore productive. They worked, paid taxes, and created more jobs with every item they purchased. She was silent after that. I think that she got my drift.

Being industrious to a fault, Anna's father expected that she would get work after high school graduation and pay some room and board too. This would mean more delay for her to get married. Anna was furious when she heard this. She responded that her father was in America for nine years and didn't contribute to her living during that time. He then threatened not to consent to her getting married. Since she was on the verge of turning twenty-one on September 6th, she did not actually need his consent. With everything else in order, we just had to wait until this date. Tensions began to cool off and with Rachel's intervention, things smoothed over slowly. Anna's father had to accept the idea after all. Finally he agreed to walk her down the aisle the day of the wedding.

Rachel, Anna, and I would pay for most of the expenses. That was a weight off of his shoulders. Ralph was known for being tight with money. I guess you can kind of understand why. He endured so much during such hard times.

As the wedding date got closer, the wedding party was selected. It consisted of all of my father's cousins' sons from Eastern Ohio. One of them was my best man. Tino, my mentor from eighth grade, was in the wedding party also. Anna selected most of the bridesmaids and her maid of honor. This was the moment I waited for, yet I was somewhat apprehensive. We went for pre-marriage instructions from the local priest, who would eventually say the mass and perform the wedding ceremony. This was to be a happy occasion, but a somber one too. Two individuals were pledging their lives to one another with no deposit and no return. It was a matter of "for better or worse, as long as you both shall live." Divorce was a topic that was not even considered by us. Marriage was a commitment for life. We pledged to make it work no matter what. That is how we both were raised. That is why we were able to connect so well with each other and make the marriage work.

When we both recited the vows, it was with conviction. We looked one another in the eyes and we both shed tears. For the first time in my life, I felt as though I had someone to trust, someone who will be there for me through it all. When we walked back down the aisle to the back of the church, Jen, Uncle Anthony's wife (I called all my father's cousins "uncle" out of respect), said to Anna, "Take care of him -- you're all he's got." We both cried real tears after that comment. We knew she was right. This marriage was for keeps.

Looking back at it all it was crazy how the boy that Zia Concetta went to help deliver in 1936, the one whom she said to her neighbor Rachel "what a big head he had," had now married Rachel's daughter, who at that time was yet to be born for two more years. It's just incredible, really.

I remember Anna as this little girl acting kind of reserved near our school when I was about twelve. I had looked at her, knowing who she was, but not knowing what she was all about. I had tried to figure out if she was the city type or more of a country person. I never did decide that while in Italy. On one hand, she did hang out with the city girls and was taking sartorial interests to heart, though I was not aware of it at the time. But her grandfather and her brother Joseph did work the farm land. After coming to America, it didn't make a difference anymore. That old way of thinking didn't mean anything anymore to me.

The first time that I visited the Conti family in 1953, Anna was fifteen and I was seventeen. I did think that she might grow up to be quite a catch. However, I didn't give it too much attention until more than five years later. She had grown into a beautiful young lady. Somehow I knew that she would be someone with whom I would not mind settling down -- and settle we did. We were a good match for one another.

After we were married, she wanted to start a family soon. By our first anniversary we already had one child about a month old. By our fourth anniversary we added two more. Then after a pause of almost six years, we added one more. Family was always a priority for us.

We had some tough times but mostly we got along and made it work. I came to realize that she was the one I needed in my life. As she also admits, I was equally the one she needed in her life. We came to the conclusion that God had a lot to do with bringing us together. There were too many things that fell into place for it to be a matter of fate, destiny, or even coincidence.

This past September 12, 2014, we celebrated our 55th wedding anniversary. It's hard to believe so much time has passed. There are a lot of memories tucked in between those 55 years.

Chapter 11: Defining Moments

Soon after we got married, I decided to let go of the job that I had taken from Tino, the one with the Italian bread company. This allowed me to no longer have to drive to Ohio every morning and then drive back to Western Pennsylvania at the end of my work day. What a relief that was for me.

I did have a nostalgic attachment to that old route. It was called the "country route." It paid $76 per week and no commission. Its design was not to supply the large chain stores in the Youngstown area, since the companies had other stores scattered throughout the surrounding small communities in Eastern Ohio and Western Pennsylvania. The purpose was actually to help the mega stores in the large community of the Youngstown area. It was a huge help and convenience for the mega stores as they had stores in these small communities also. The money wasn't bad for the amount of work I had to do each day. When I would come back from the route, someone would check my account against the load that I took out that day. After that, I was free to go home. It worked well while I lived in Eastern Ohio, but it became a huge burden once I moved to Western Pennsylvania.

I took another job for a major baking company in my hometown in New Castle, Pennsylvania. The money was better but the hours were long and tedious. Unlike the first job where I had only large and small loaves and buns, this new job had hundreds of items to sell. Not that I carried them every day, but I had to check these going into stores and again when I took these back out of stores.

After finishing my route each day, I checked my returns with someone at the local office. Then I checked myself in against a settlement sheet. If I was short or off on the balance sheet, then more time had to be spent until I found my shortage. In some instances, I had to put money in from my own pocket to balance things out. In summary, I could put in anywhere from 10 to 14 hours per day. We ordered our own loads of goods two or more days in advance. Then, we recorded what we returned against what we had ordered in a book. It was crazy, especially when we had large amounts of returns. It meant that we not only had a lot of goods to take back, but we made no money on our returns.

This job was wearing me out. I remember dozing off watching TV in the evenings. When my wife called me to go to bed, I once responded with "How many dozens of buns do you want?" Then there were times when the weather was bad and it was close to impossible to make the route. I had to lie under my truck and put chains on in the frigid cold. I thought my hands and fingers would fall off my arms. But when you have a wife, kids, and a house payment, somehow you find the courage and stamina to endure.

One evening, I was going to be late getting home and told my wife to go ahead and let the children eat. Later, as I was eating supper by myself, I fell asleep and my face fell into the supper dish. I knew then that I had to find a new job. I started to look for one immediately. I thought maybe a factory job where I would work eight hours and then go home was more humane. At least if I needed to use the restroom, there was one nearby. On the route, sometimes I couldn't even stop because I had deadlines to be at certain stores or restaurants. They depended on us to be there on time or lose their business for good. The pressure was enormous.

I heard that the local Rockwell plant in New Castle was hiring. After a couple tries I was hired. The work was hard but they paid me well and included good health benefits. Being new, I had to work a lot of overtime. No refusing was allowed. The only difference was that I earned much more with overtime and time and a half Saturday and double time on Sundays. The health insurance was much better than I had hoped. After more than six years of driver sales I joined the Rockwell workforce and began a new chapter in my life.

My first job was as a shipper, working three to eleven PM. Even though I was putting in just as many hours as the day shift, I was happier. Soon we had another child and that made a total of four: two boys and two girls.

Eventually, I moved on to being a machine operator and earned a little extra. After I found my way around the plant, I moved up to quality inspector. Through quality control we tested parts for defects with a process called magnetic particle testing. Years later, when the plant was expanding for a time, there arose a need for metallurgic technicians. I applied for this group and after some intensive and crammed studying, I passed the required testing. I continued to work in that capacity for several years and made better pay along the way.

Earlier, when I was still a machine operator, I became involved with the local United Steel Workers (USW) union. I served three years as treasurer and along with that job I was appointed head of the political action committee. This position allowed me to travel to many conferences with the president of the union and other members. We worked and lobbied for legislation favorable to labor. We worked on such matters at the state level as well as at the federal level.

There were a lot of things we addressed concerning the care of the workers. Sometimes it was about health insurance issues. Other times it was about a variety of other issues. Sometimes it was about tariffs on subsidized steel imports from other countries that were dumped on our shore at a cost below what our American steel mills could produce. This was due to the fact that some other nations subsidized steel production in their countries. At this time in my life, I was still a registered Democrat.

In 1974, just after President Nixon resigned due to the Watergate scandal, I experienced one of the most memorable moments of my life. It concerned the issue of pension reform. This was a hot topic in the sixties and early seventies. We had been lobbying our US Senators as well as our local Congressmen. Up to that point, companies would often close plants and then raid the pension funds of the former employees. Then they would move out of state or sell the company off. The poor retirees were left without a job or pension. So we went to

Washington several times en masse to fight for the reform of this practice.

After all our hard work, something amazing happened. President Ford took office and we were gratified when he signed the Pension Reform Act into law. I'll never forget it. I was traveling in my car. It was Labor Day of 1974 when the news broke that Ford signed this law. It gave me a sense of satisfaction. From now on, if you had a pension while on the job, you could count on receiving it when you retired. The fact that I had been a part of making that happen made me so proud to be an American. To come from war torn Europe and face so many hardships, to now meeting with members of the US Congress and influencing their decisions was simply amazing.

I worked at that Rockwell plant for 27 years in all. I planned to work there longer but the plant finally closed in 1993. They dispersed our work to other plants around the country. Faced with the decision to be bumped into another department while the plant was closing own, where there was heavy work and a lot of smoke, I decided to take an offer to retire early at fifty-seven years of age. I was confident that I could make it in the work force.

At first it was not very easy. I had to take a job in a tool and die shop earning very little pay. There were a few hard years. Then a break came my way. Because of my early sales experience as a driver/salesman, I was able to get a job as a family counselor with a major cemetery company that owned about eighteen cemeteries in the tri-state area of Ohio, Pennsylvania, and West Virginia. At first I wasn't sure that I could make a living doing this type of work. It was a commission based pay. But with training I began to like the job. Having worked in a factory for almost twenty-seven years, often seven days per week with overtime, it made my sales job a breeze.

When I really think about it, my job at Rockwell was the best thing that could have happened to my career. Financially, it was a real blessing. However, my body was breaking down from the repeated hard work, stress, and strain. I am sure all of that overtime I worked was taking a toll on me. My body didn't have time to recover as I jumped right into the work force after my time at Rockwell. I developed carpal tunnel syndrome in both wrists and all my fingers developed trigger finger. Thankfully, surgery did repair all of the damage in the end. I did carry other scars too. I still carry a small hardened steel chip in my chest and lost a patch of skin over my collar bone. Overall, I came through without any serious injury.

When I started my new sales job, I felt very good about what I did. I helped people pre-arrange for the next life. I made many friends that I still see sometimes. I was honest with everyone. Sometimes I bent over backwards to make them happy. I enjoyed seeing people happy. That gave me a high. Many appreciated my honesty and service. Soon people would send their friends to me. I had so much fun doing it. I was even rewarded with a trip for my wife and I to vacation in the Bahamas, all paid by my company. I was able to work until I was well over retirement age. Then I worked for a few years with that same company on a part-time basis. I think that those were my best and happiest years working. In the end, in my final sale, I sold a private estate to an elderly woman. It was all polished granite, truly a beautiful building. However, when she died, her niece and husband refused to build it. They threatened to sue. A settlement was finally reached. I still made my commission of about a year's wage. It was a fulfilling wrap up to my working career.

Sometimes I look back and everything seems surreal. My family slowly has died off and is no more. My two brothers who I lost when I was young will always be young in my memory. Leo will certainly be in my mind most of all. I never forget that moment when I stood in front of his crypt. There was something that happened that day that gave me closure.

Then there is Al -- or Alfonso. I hear his voice on the "International Hour" every Saturday when I hear the songs he used to sing, now coming through the airwaves when I listen to the radio and songs of that era. Then, I am a child again, full of innocence and awe. I am brought back to the locale where I was when I last saw him. I can see my surroundings. I can smell the fresh air and see the sunny hills and countryside all in harmony with each other. I can taste a bit of home. It is something to experience. When I try to describe it, words alone can't capture the essence of what I feel. I imagine that everyone has a similar experience at one time or another.

We were all at one time children and innocent, full of wonder. This is what I remember about my time growing up. That is until the war began and everything seemed to spin out of control. Those struggles and the suffering that came later are part of my life and have made me who I am. You know, we all have a story in us. It may be different from mine, but that is not important. I think it is important to share your story for whatever it might be worth. We can all grow from each other's story.

All I can say is: God bless America. It has a rich history. Too many have given up their lives to make it what it is. We should preserve it so that the future generations can have a taste of what we have enjoyed.

I must say, I think that our Constitution and form of government is the best of all the others on this planet. The founding fathers endured many hardships and sufferings as they were oppressed by the British Empire. Out of that suffering came a better form of government. Just like them, I have learned that with hard work and determination you can overcome many adversities and still succeed.

Looking back on things, I have to say that one of my biggest regrets in life was when I met President Eisenhower face to face on that ship, but did not thank him for liberating the Italian people from Mussolini -- and from the Germans who had taken over parts of Italy after the signing of the Armistice with the Allies.

Call me crazy, but I think this shepherd boy has succeeded in life. I may not have become a millionaire or even a famous man. I did not achieve great feats or make any discoveries. Things have not always gone my way. I have not always won, but I played the game. Just as the lottery ads say, "You must play to win." This applies to life as well.

I am proud to have been an American citizen for all of these years, even if part of me can't forget my country of origin. After all, you cannot erase your past, even if you try. I love both cultures and feel richer for it. I enjoy songs and music from both cultures and enjoy knowing both languages. I was grateful to participate in the political process while a member of the steel workers union. Although I am now a registered Republican, I still believe that the pension reform we supported back in the 1970's was important.

I have been back many times to visit my old country. I have always enjoyed my stays there. I still have close relatives back in Italy, but I am always glad to come back to America. Only in America can a shepherd boy immigrate and in a few short years complete his high school education, serve his new country honorably, rise through the ranks as an E-4, meet the President who liberated his home town from the Nazis, and then raise a family of six and retire as a metallurgical technician with a major industrial giant. Lest I forget, I could not have done everything without the woman I married. She was and is a great influence on my life.

In retrospect, looking at the obstacles and hardships I had to endure, I think that I have no reason to be ashamed. I never asked for a handout. I hope that this does not sound like bragging. I know that I did not split the atom or find a cure for cancer. Yet, if a shepherd boy can overcome so many obstacles, then those born in this great country of ours should be encouraged to accomplish much greater things than me. We have to look only to the Pilgrims and how hard they had it. First they took great risks crossing the Atlantic with the wooden ships of the day. Then they faced cold winters without proper housing and heating. Plumbing didn't even exist. Food shortages and diseases abounded. Many died just to have the opportunity for a better life.

Then there were the frontiersmen. Many died just to get to the frontier. The ones that made it to the west faced many problems. When I read of their suffering and sacrifices, I am humbled and ashamed to complain about anything. The immigrants who came before me are the ones that built the bridges and the infrastructure of the nation. They are the ones that have allowed us to enjoy the freedom and good things that the country gives us. They are the ones deserving of our praise. Having endured the peril and dangers of disease, hardship, and the loss of life, they prepared a land for us like no other. It is a rich and fertile land that can feed all its inhabitants and still export to other countries around the world. They put in motion a great nation using their foresight and innovation.

I remember as a young boy in the old country, two pounds of beans, if you did not grow it on your own, would cost you a day's wage. The same went for a pair of leather shoes for the winter. You saw the doctor only if you were on the verge of death. I have to admit that not everyone was in that situation. However, the majority of people who worked the land were often in that category.

When I first came to this nation, I felt like a stranger. As time passed and my family grew, I started to feel more and more that I belonged here. This is my lasting home. I am fine with that. However, now that my family in Italy is all gone, I miss them terribly. I realize that I spent too little time with them. I would have liked for my parents to share in the joy when Anna and I got married and when my children were born. Any parent knows the joy of having children.

Things have improved greatly in Italy since WWII. In America, even in the 19th century and earlier, people had better living conditions. My parents knew this. I had to choose America over my homeland. Sure it was hard for me to leave part of my life there. But America had introduced the world to many things, of which the rest of the world was envious. I wanted those things for my family, for myself and my children. I had to think of my future.

I mentioned some important items that America offered. Now I'd like to touch on some less important but still significant goodies. America has given the world famous novelties like Coca-Cola and Pepsi Cola. I found Coca-Cola in the most remote places while serving in the Navy. America also gave us chewing gum, western movies, potato chips, hamburgers, french fries, hot dogs, baseball, and many other things the world enjoys. Lest I forget, the other important thing America has given to the world is freedom from oppression, not only in WWI and WWII, but in many other conflicts. Best of all, it has never conquered any land to keep as a colony of war. In fact, wherever it has fought, it has established democracy and has enriched each nation by leaving it in better condition than before. We have to look only to Germany for an example. Their economy is the envy of Europe. Japan is another example. Look at the sharp contrast between North Korea and South Korea. An aerial view of North and South Korea at night shows an amazing contrast. South Korea is fully illuminated with lights, but North Korea is totally dark. This is what the power of freedom can do to a nation.

The reason Europe prospered after the Second World War is because America maintained stability there. The American military bases that are still there today have given Europe time to grow, all the while unprovoked from aggression of neighboring countries. This was not the case in the past before America's influence.

Europe has changed immensely with the help of America. The standard of living has risen in Europe. Travel between nations is now very easy. Commerce and ideas between nations are encouraged. There are more businesses opening up everywhere.

You know, the last two times I visited Italy, I saw with my own eyes the progress they have made. People that had been abroad working returned with capital and new ideas. They built new factories, opened shops, and offered new items. All this and more and it all stemmed from the stability of governments that came by way of American influence.

There in Italy, I saw people that had immigrated from Poland and other freed states. They came to work as maids and nannies. This was unheard of a few decades ago. People immigrate to places that offer better living wages and a higher standard of living. There were people there from as far as India, Africa, and many other places. The fields that my family once worked along with some hired laborers are now being worked by tractors and other modern machinery. The crops that we used to harvest once per season are now harvested two to three times per year. This was made possible through a series of channels built far upstream on the river. They split the river in half and channeled it through a mountain with a tunnel. From there, channels bring water to irrigate ditches that traverse the countryside. This makes their farming drought-proof. The corn stalks are now eight to ten feet high. When I was growing up this was not even possible. We planted one crop of corn, one of wheat, and so on. We prayed that the weather would cooperate so we would yield a good measure of each crop. Even with good weather our yield was average. Now with irrigation and better fertilizers, the crops are much higher and more plentiful. Plus, they get at least two, if not three, crops per year.

The earlier populations in Italy knew war and destruction. With peace and stability, everyone benefits through cooperation and good will. Once again, we have to credit this mostly to America for maintaining peace in Europe. No other major power could afford to lend this vast kind of protection to the free world.

I have learned the cost of freedom isn't free. It comes at a high price. Freedom itself is so taken for granted. Having lived through a major world war, I can tell you that it is worth preserving. Freedom is the difference between living life to the full and simply existing. That is why we must be vigilant and ready to fight for our freedoms. We do not want to destroy ourselves as many are doing in their own countries. The last thing we should do is reverse all that we know and have accomplished in over two centuries. Unfortunately, I fear that many young people do not appreciate all that America stands for and represents to the world.

I have to give credit to former Italian Premier Berlusconi. When he spoke to the United States Congress some years ago, he recounted the story that his father had told him. When he graduated from either high school or college, his father took him to an American cemetery where Americans who fought in WW II were buried in Italy. His father told his son to never forget the sacrifice that these American soldiers made to liberate Italy and most of Europe. No other country has made this sacrifice for Europe, in either the First World War or the Second World War. If it wasn't for America, many Europeans would be under Nazi control. If it wasn't for America, many others would be under communist control. I think about these things now in my late seventies.

My last visit to Italy was in the summer of 2012. I felt somewhat like a stranger there instead of a stranger in America, like I did during my teenage years. When I used to walk in town on earlier visits to Italy, I could still see people I knew. This last visit, I felt that when I walked around town, people had no clue that I was from there. They seemed to ignore me. But I know that this was not true. They were just looking at a person they didn't know. They were just not aware that I too had lived and played there and walked the piazzas as they do today. I wanted to say to the people there, "Hey, don't you know me? I walked these streets before you were born. I attended school in the same buildings that are still in use. I see the same hills and panoramic view."

Most buildings are still standing in my hometown. The roads are modified and some homes and buildings have been modernized, but I can recognize them for what they used to be. It is a part of my past, but I see you in my mind's eye when I hear "Canzoni Italiane," the Italian songs on the Italian program on WKTL in Struthers, Ohio, every Saturday from 3 p.m. to 4:30 p.m.

I doubt that I will ever visit Italy again. Health and age changes a person. My concern now is to take care of my wife as she has taken care of me all these years. She is the one who breathed new life into me when I needed someone the most. She has been the reason for my longevity. At one time, I was under a lot of stress. I used to think that I would have a heart attack by thirty-five years of age. Well, I missed it by ten years. At forty-five years of age I did have one. I used to smoke from an early age. That didn't help matters. I survived the heart attack and two open heart surgeries for by-passes. She was there for me. Now that we are getting older and needier, I want to be there for her too.

Travel used to be easy at one time. Nowadays, with all the rules and regulations after 9/11, I am more hesitant to travel. Then, there is the lugging of personal effects through longer terminals. Another thing we must calculate is the prescription medications we need to take along with us. We need to be sure we have enough for the period of time that we are away. Then there is the packing. All this can become a heavy burden. So home seems more desirable now. Besides, if you are happy, you can be happy anywhere. If you are miserable, you will be miserable no matter where you visit.

As a young man, being brought up in a rural environment, I had time to observe nature. There were animals of all kinds, domesticated and wild. I also learned to read weather patterns because they affected my life and the life of nature. I had time to observe the heavens. I lived mostly in open air most days of my young life.

One day, when I was about nine years old, I looked up at the clouds in the sky. I thought of heavenly bodies such as stars, the moon, constellations, comets, an occasional moon eclipse, and the nearest star, our sun. I realized that humans were not up there directing things and making things happen with our skills or intervention

-- or physically putting things in motion. It was a supernatural order that no man could ever master on his own -- let alone order the events and great manifestations to take place at will. These were fixed by a supernatural being with knowledge beyond human capabilities. Therefore, I knew then there has to be a supernatural being -- God.

In my later years, I have experienced God in my life personally and found him to be awesome. While I do not want to come across sounding like a preacher, I have come to value spiritual things rather than worldly things. I value my wife and the four children that we had together. She has always made me proud and still does. I have come to value my health. Now at age 78, I have to ask how did all of this -- my crazy life -- just happen? It was not by accident. Sure, I had to do my part. But ultimately my prayers have been answered many times. I could not have done it on my own. There were periods of time when I had to fight my demons, as we all do. But rest assured that with divine intervention I was able to get through it all. God does answer the prayers of those who seek Him with a sincere heart. My life is proof of that.

I will never forget October of 1982. I was in the hospital the night before my first by-pass heart surgery. I was talking with some other patients. One asked me if I was fearful. Later, when I turned in for the night, all alone there, things did go through my mind as they would for anyone before an event of such magnitude.

As I searched my thoughts, I remembered that I had made preparations just in case. I had gone to confession and made peace with God for all that I had done wrong in my life. I received an anointing for the sick from my priest who prayed for my recovery. As I pondered these thoughts, I realized that if I died after having confessed my sins to God and shown remorse for them, I would have gone to heaven. And if I survived, I would be much healthier. So what did I have to fear? I could win in both instances. Therefore, there was no more reason to fear.

Much later, after I recovered, I visited a family friend who had the terrible disease of cancer. As we talked, this person was very afraid of dying from the disease. I thought about what I could say to ease the anguish in her heart. Then, the thought crossed my mind. Perhaps I could share my experience when in the hospital of being ready spiritually to meet my maker. Whether this person chose to heed my encouragement or not, I cannot be sure.

But I know that if I was in the same situation, it would at the very least be of some comfort to me.

One day some years ago, I was down in the dumps and learned another lesson. I happened to go to Walmart. There I saw a young man in a wheel chair. He had some sort of paralysis. I was so ashamed about being depressed about my own problems. I resolved to quit feeling that way. There is always another person worse off somewhere. I decided to cheer up and thank God for what I had. I could not change the past. I could only be thankful for the present.

Sometimes we miss the forest for the trees. We seem to forget that God is willing to protect us if we will just reach out for Him; that includes you as well. That, my friends, is an awesome thing to have -- the security and peace of mind that comes with clearing your conscience and resting in God's hand of protection.

I must not forget that through all that I have accomplished and endured in life, I could not have done it alone. There was divine intervention in all of the major accomplishments and undertakings. Therefore, I must give God credit and thanks. I trust that with His grace, we will reach the Promised Land someday. Without that hope in mind, life would be an exercise in futility. I hope to reunite with my family someday in the other life where there will be rejoicing and laughter. It's my sincere wish for all people.

I have concluded that time is the enemy that divides us. It creeps up on us and we can't remember where it all went, especially when you get to be my age. The good news is that you can overcome difficulties if you have the right perspective on things. You can never discount that invisible hand of God that seeks to guide and direct you. You just have to be willing to give Him a chance to show you what your life can be. You have to make the choice to receive the gift of His direction.

I must say good-bye for now. These are the memories and lives that I left behind. They have made me who I am and I will carry them into the next life one of these days. Ciao.

Appendix

The role of the Third Infantry Division in liberating the town of Baia during WW II:

On July 10, 1943, the Third Infantry Division landed in Sicily near a town called Licata. The division had to fight its way into Palermo without their armored support, as it had not yet arrived. They kept moving and quickly captured Messina, bringing an end to the US military's Sicilian campaign.

On September 18, 1943, the division arrived at Salerno. From there they faced heavy fire from the enemy but pressed on. They made a massive push toward Cassino and crossed the Volturno River (the river that runs through Baia) in October of 1943. It was some short time after this that they liberated the town of Baia from the Nazi occupation that had taken root there.

Moving on to Cassino in early 1944, the division would later engage in the battle of Monte Cassino, which was an intense and long battle that lasted from January of 1944 until May of 1944.

During WW II, a total of 4,922 soldiers of the Third Infantry Division were killed in action. 18,766 soldiers of the division were wounded.

Made in the USA
Columbia, SC
26 September 2020